# The Years of the Locust

Jon Hotten is the author of *Unlicensed* and *Muscle*.

Also by Jon Hotten

*Unlicensed:*
*Random Notes from Boxing's Underbelly*

*Muscle:*
*A Writer's Trip Through a Sport with no Boundaries*

# The Years of
# the Locust

*A True Story of Murder, Money and
Mayhem in the Last Age of Boxing*

**Jon Hotten**

Yellow Jersey Press
LONDON

Published by Yellow Jersey Press 2009

2 4 6 8 10 9 7 5 3 1

First published in Great Britain in 2009 by
Yellow Jersey Press
Random House, 20 Vauxhall Bridge Road,
London SW1V 2SA

www.rbooks.co.uk

Addresses for companies within
The Random House Group Limited
can be found at:
www.randomhouse.co.uk/offices.htm

The Random House Group Limited Reg. No. 954009

A CIP catalogue record for this book
is available from the British Library

ISBN 9780224080262

The Random House Group Limited supports The Forest Stewardship Council
(FSC), the leading international forest certification organisation. All our titles
that are printed on Greenpeace approved FSC certified paper carry the FSC
logo. Our paper procurement policy can be found at
www.rbooks.co.uk/environment

**Mixed Sources**
Product group from well-managed
forests and other controlled sources
www.fsc.org  Cert no. TT-COC-2139
© 1996 Forest Stewardship Council

FSC

Printed and bound in Great Britain by
Clays Ltd, St Ives PLC

*To Yasmin*

# Contents

# List of Characters

**The protagonists**

Rick Parker, aka Rick 'Elvis' Parker, Fat Rick – cleaning
  sales king turned boxing promoter
Tim Anderson, aka 'Doc' Anderson – former baseball pro,
  now a heavyweight boxer

**Rick's family**

Diane McVay – Rick's half-sister and occasional
  business partner
Chris Parker – Rick's son
Holly – Rick's girlfriend

**Tim's family**

George Anderson – Tim's father
Jacqueline Anderson, née Mundo – Tim's mother
Erin Anderson – Tim's sister
Darrin and Tommy Anderson – Tim's younger brothers

## The boxers

Smokin' Bert Cooper, aka $50 Bert – heavyweight contender
George Foreman – former heavyweight champion of the world
Randall 'Tex' Cobb – great white hope and part-time actor
Mark Gastineau – linebacker for the New York Jets turned great white hope
Evander Holyfield – heavyweight champion of the world
Paul 'Sonny' Barch – white heavyweight boxer
Rick Hoard – white heavyweight boxer
Frank Lux, aka Frank Williams/Frankie Albert, a white heavyweight
Pierre Coetzer – white South African heavyweight
Houston Perkins – boxer and referee
Derrick 'Starfire' Dukes – professional wrestler turned boxer (for one fight only)
Mitch 'Blood' Green – maverick heavyweight once promoted by Rick Parker

## The businessmen

Don King – boxing promoter; Rick Parker's hero
Bob Arum – Don King's long-time professional rival, founder of Top Rank Boxing
Don Hazelton – Florida State Athletic Commissioner
Dan Duva – boxing promoter, brother of Lou, a trainer
Rob Russen – Rick's business partner in Rick Parker Presents . . .
Doug Davis – bar owner
Sean Gibbons – matchmaker
Pete Susens – matchmaker
Joe Derrick – Tex Cobb's manager
Ron Weathers – boxing manager of Tex Cobb and George Foreman

## The lawyers

Ellis Rubin – Tim Anderson's first lawyer
Bill McClellan – public defender representing Tim Anderson
Patricia Cashman – public defender representing Tim Anderson
Dorothy Sedgwick – public prosecutor in Tim Anderson's case
Richard Conrad – Orange County Circuit Judge

## Also . . .

Jim Murphy – Tim Anderson's best friend
Sharon Cobb, née Hodge – Tex Cobb's (then) wife and a journalist
Randy Gerber – publicist for the George Foreman–Tim Anderson fight
Steve Benson – publicist for the Fort Lauderdale bill of 1992
Steve Canton – boxing trainer and friend of Tim Anderson's
Mary Lynn Canton – Steve's (then) wife and Tim's friend
Denis Jones – Rick Parker's driver
Ken Rodriguez – journalist with the *Miami Herald*
Steve Kroft – presenter of the CBS *60 Minutes* television show
Richard Smitten – writer, friend of Ellis Rubin
Suzanne Migdall – owner of Summers On The Beach nightclub, movie producer and former manager of Tim
Steve Thomasson – boxing referee
Ken Knox – writer with *Boxing Illustrated* magazine

## Rick Parker's businesses

American Safety Industries – cleaning sales company selling products door to door, principally The Green Cleaner, aka 'the Green' or Sun-Sation
Rick Parker Presents . . . – his boxing promotions company

'Yesterday I was lying. Today, I'm telling the truth'

Bob Arum, boxing promoter

Arcane fragments of Richard Lynn Parker remain in this world. The bullets that ended his life lie in a long-closed drawer, dead evidence of old crimes. On their casings, the final traces of atomised soft tissue, the very last of his DNA. His own gun, the silver Glock automatic, has never been found. The houses he lived in still stand; walls he has touched, doors he has closed. Even his fucking hairpiece should be somewhere. But what's left most is his story, the story of the worst man you never knew. That story reverberates in Tim Anderson, and in others, too. Rick Parker, for them, still lives, massed and near, if now just out of sight.

# Prologue

*28 April 1995.* So here he comes, Fat Rick Parker, rocking and rolling through Orlando International Airport on this, the last day of his life. Black slacks and a red sports coat. A floral shirt and cowboy boots. The great red hairpiece on his head. The boxing glove charm around his neck. The Glock automatic in its holster by his boot, strapped on tight to his fat white leg.

Past the baggage claim and out of the hall, down the stairs and through the doors, into the heat and into the light, he sits alone in the back of the cab. Up the curving freeway ramp, under the early summer sun, his silver briefcase on his lap.

Fat Rick sees the EZ Pawn store from two blocks away. He calls the driver to a stop. Out of the cab and into the heat. Through the door and into the shop. Up to the till and off with the necklace. The solid gold glove on its solid gold chain. He weighs it in his fat right hand.

Renee is the name of the woman behind the counter. Renee takes the charm and weighs it up. She puts a loop to her eye and examines the marks. She lays it out and measures its length. Twenty-two inches and tight around his neck. She places it on her cloth and gives it a rub. No genie comes, no magic rises. Not for Rick Parker, not today.

'Two hundred and twenty,' she says.

'Uh, sure, honey,' says Rick Parker.

'Can I do anything else for you?'

He thinks of the gun in its holster by his boot. The Glock automatic strapped to his leg.

'No, ma'am, not right now.'

She writes out his ticket and counts out his money. He places the bills and the ticket in his wallet.

'I'll be back, yes, ma'am, I will.'

Out of the shop and into the cab. Up the curving freeway ramp. The bright sun on the hard concrete. His days in boxing, on his mind. One punch away from the Heavyweight Championship of the World.

One. Punch. Away.

Rick Parker and Bert Cooper. Fat Rick and $50 Bert, separated from the life of their dreams by one swing of Bert's magic right hand.

$50 Bert, who lived in a mobile home and spent his money on junk. $50 Bert, who might have been great.

One. Punch. Away. 23 November 1991. Never again so close. Never again able to stick it to them: Dan Duva and Don Hazelton, Bob Arum and Don King. The doubters and the gloaters. The haters and the jokers who took his money and shut him out, shut him out and shut him up, sent him away, sent him away until today: 28 April 1995.

He watches Orlando from the window of the cab. This city of swamps and freeway ramps. This city of hotels and outlet malls. This city of light, this city of heat. On I-4 in the afternoon traffic, driving towards the dipping sun, the impassive driver picking at his nails, the radio tuned to the eighties hits. Bands Rick knows. Songs he sings.

Crawling towards exit 68. Down the ramp and off the freeway. Through the traffic lights and past the gift shops, along the side street with its island of trees, up the driveway of the Embassy Suites. He pays the fare and picks up his case. He straightens his jacket and primps up his hair. Through the doors and into the hotel. Up to the desk by the dipping palms. He takes a suite overlooking the pool and pays in full, cash in advance. He registers under the name 'Jim Nelson' and gives an address in Memphis, Tennessee. First floor, room 250. He puts down the case and turns on the TV. He takes off his jacket and picks up the phone. He makes the calls that he has to make.

'Hey, it's Rick, baby . . .'

'It's Rick.'

'It's Rick Parker.'

'It's Elvis, baby. It's Elvis. Oh yeah, I'm back, that's right.'

In the bathroom of a house on the other side of town, Tim Anderson runs wet hands through blond hair and stares in the mirror. He doesn't look like a heavyweight boxer any more. More like a skinny middleweight with a glassy jaw, the kind of guy you find at the bottom of the card slipping punches for a couple of hundred bucks. He pulls off his T-shirt. His body looks like Iggy Pop's. His body *feels* like Iggy Pop's. Loose skin once filled with muscle. He puts on a tracksuit, black with white flashes on the sides. Even doing that takes some effort.

He knows who has done this to him: Rick Parker. Rick Parker and his fixed boxing matches and his poisoned water. That's about all he does know. He goes back into the bedroom, takes yellow index cards from his bag and begins to write. He writes to his father, to his sister, to his brothers, to his girlfriend. The words are different in each, but the message is the same. He takes his Bible and places the cards inside it. He digs back in the bag and brings out a gun. He takes a handful of cartridges and loads five into the chambers. The rest he shoves into his tracksuit pocket. He has never fired a gun in his life. He tucks it into the waistband of his sweatpants, at the back, and pulls the jacket down over it. He takes a dictating machine with a fresh tape inside and pushes it into the jacket pocket that doesn't have the bullets in.

'Hey, Diane,' he says. 'You ready?'

Rick Parker's voice is high and querulous. Not like Don King's. Not like Bob Arum's. A little like Elvis Presley's in accent and tone. A little like Elvis, with the voice and the hair. He sits by the pool at the Embassy Suites. He makes good use of the courtesy phone. He makes the calls he has to make. He lets them know he's still alive.

The boxing business, all laid out. That dirty, lovely business that he wanted so much. The money it cost and the pain it brought him. The joy it carried and the hope it gave him. The men who came and the men who left him. The men who fought and the men who lost. The men who believed and the men who did not.

*One. Punch. Away. The Windfall Factor. Millions and millions of dollars, all at one time.*

*Rick Parker, in control of the Heavyweight Championship of the World.*

*Don King on his knees before him. Bob Arum on his knees before him. Dan Duva on his knees before him.*

*One punch away.*

Fat Rick remembers the last words that Don King ever spoke to him – 'Fuck you, Rick Parker.'

Yeah? Well, fuck you right back, Don. And fuck you all.

He knows where he is. He knows where he will be.

Rick Parker, rising again.

Rick Parker, rising.

Rick Parker rising.

Fat Rick calls around seven. He's at the Embassy Suites in Lake Buena Vista. Room 250. First floor, past the bar, by the pool. Just walk right up. Now Tim Anderson is in a car with Rick's sister Diane and Rick's son Chris, who is fourteen years old and hasn't seen Rick in two years, maybe more. None of them has. Diane is driving. Tim sits in the front passenger seat. He's tucked his Bible under his seat. He can feel the hard edges of the gun in the small of his back. He is more afraid of killing than of dying. He is dying anyway, has been since Rick Parker slipped him tainted water before the fight in Oklahoma City. His mind is full. He no longer knows if he is sane or not. He talks to Diane about their days on the road, all those years ago, selling 'the Green' and dreaming of glory. He tells Chris what his father has done to him.

They arrive at the Embassy Suites and walk through the atrium with its dipping palms.

Rick sees them first through the frosted glass. He smiles to himself and flips the catch. Chris got older, taller. Tim got thinner, smaller. He swings the door wide and he welcomes them in. Out of the heat and out of the night, into the cool twilight of his hotel room. They hug and they kiss. They sit down and talk. They laugh and remember. Diane takes out her camera. When they're done, Tim whispers something and Diane takes Chris by the hand and says, 'Chris, let these two men talk their business. We'll take a walk around the hotel.' Rick lets them out.

And now they are alone.

Rick lies on the floor, on his back beside the bed, bullets in him and through him. So this was it; here it was at last. Big Tim, big, dumb, loyal Tim, of all the people it might have been.

'Oh, Doc, you stupid . . .' he thinks he says. 'C'mon, buddy

. . . c'mon, my old buddy . . . let's make lemonade . . . Let's make lemonade out of this lemon . . .'

Later, as he recedes, through the glass panel by the door he sees Chris looking in. He raises his head and then he lays it down. His son looks back through the glass and then tries to get the door open, panic in his eyes, a sickness in his heart, knowing but not knowing, knowing but not wanting to know.

# Part One

# First and Last

Rick Parker (*left*) with Mitch 'Blood' Green, *c.*1992
(*courtesy Rob Russen*)

# Fat Rick and Sneaky Pete

*I*magine *how it was, opening your door to find Mr Richard Lynn Parker standing there on your driveway with his plastic drum of Sun-Sation in one fat hand and his silver case in the other, the sun beating down in Missouri or Tennessee or wherever the hell you are today . . .*

*'G'morning, sir', or 'Good morning, ma'am' you hear in that Southern sing-song voice. 'I think I have something here that can help you . . .' You find yourself aware of the charge of his presence, not just from his size, although he's undoubtedly bigger than you, not just from his clothes or his towering hair, but from the way he makes you feel that somehow, you need to help him.*

*Imagine how it was to have him go through his act of finding some dirt on your carpets or some oil on your driveway or if not finding some putting it there, and then miraculously cleaning it off with the Sun-Sation, which he then sells you for the rock-bottom, one-time-only price of whatever it is, which seems really low while he's standing there and then somewhat higher when he's gotten back in his car and left the neighbourhood with your money in his pocket. Imagine how it was when a few days later you take out your own gallon drum of Sun-Sation and apply it to the latest stain or mark or spillage and you work away for longer than you should before you stand up and you say to yourself, 'You know, this stuff the fat guy sold me isn't what I thought . . .'*

Oh, he liked the little taste of money and power he got from the cleaning company, he liked the buzz and the crackle of it. He liked the feeling of walking off the doorstep with the cash in his pocket, knowing that he'd talked it there. It was like magic, something out of nothing. For the first time in his life he was getting his due. For the first time in his life he felt like he was connecting with what he might be.

He came from Springfield, Missouri, not that it mattered. Born 24 June 1955. The creature that he would grow into arrived pissing and bawling in the prim and proper fifties, missed out on the sixties altogether, left home just as the splintered seventies began. He didn't know his father. He grew up with his mother and his half-sister Diane, who was just a tick older than he was. His mother had a business breeding guard dogs and she had night work, too, so it was Diane who raised Rick, who cleaned up his crap and made sure he had something to eat. His mother was a cold individual. There was no love and tenderness with her. Little Rick was an entrepreneur from the start. He arranged for his buddies to cut lawns and then took the money for himself. He laid his schemes and his plans. He always knew he would have to make his own way.

When he was thirteen and Diane was sixteen they moved from Springfield, Missouri, to Lakeland, Florida, right there between Plant City and Winter Haven. Diane was so desperate to get away she married a guy and moved out. Rick quit school at sixteen. The world to him looked hostile, conspiratorial. He hovered around until he found something he could do. He

found it in a bar. He found out he could shoot pool like a fucking magician. He taught himself how to play good. Then he
taught himself how to play bad. The classic lemon. It worked
like a charm. He learned how to work a small pool hall for a few
dollars. He began taking little road trips, two days here, three
days there, heading for places where they didn't know his face.
He had to. One look at Fat Rick and you never forgot him. His
curse: he could never hustle anywhere twice. He worked out
some longer cons, going to the same bar for a few weeks,
winning a little, losing more. Pulling them in until he was
ready. Lulling them and then boom . . .

*Imagine how it was to have Fat Rick turning up in your
barroom or pool hall in the first bloom of manhood, standing
there with his cue case in one hand and his dick in the other,
a red-headed orphan with no home to go to. Bumfluff on his
chin. Hair like Georgia pine straw. He shoots a few racks with
his eye on every table except the one that he's playing.*

*'Hey, buddy, fancy a game?'*

*So he starts playing these guys you know to be pretty good
and he takes money from them, not a large amount, but
something. Then they double up and he begins to lose.*

*'Hey, boys,' he says. 'I'll be in here tomorrow night. I'm
gonna win it all back from you.'*

*'Sure you will, buddy.'*

*But he is back the following night and the night after that.
He strokes them. He feeds them. Then the sting. Seems obvious
when it's written down but they don't see it coming. The
double-money match that he wins on the eight ball. The ego
bets that they can't help making.*

*'Thanks, guys. I'll be here tomorrow. You can try to get it
back from me.'*

*But he isn't and they don't. He slips from the bar and on to
the road. They'll never see him again. They'll never forget his
face.*

*'Shit,' they'll say to one another. 'That red-headed freak just took off with our money.'*

He wore out central Florida. The shaded towns by distant interstates. The dusty cities off the tourist routes. Mulbury, Bartow, Bowling Green. Bloomingdale, Avon Park, Arcadia. Vero Beach, Fort Pierce, Port St Lucie. Further north, Gainesville, Jacksonville, Lake City. Out of Florida and into Missouri, Georgia, Mississippi. Same shitty towns. Same no-mark cities. The lemon, the hustle. The car, the road.

After a year of it, he wore its look, in his clothes, on his face. He was bars and he was late nights. He was miles and he was freeways. He moved on. He evolved. The weary clothes of a travelling man. The junk-food pallor of the struggling man. All part of the show, all a part of the act.

He had a pool stick that matched his look. It was a good cue that looked like a house cue. In the hustling game they called it a Sneaky Pete. He'd drink plenty of beer and throw his money around like a crazy drunk. He'd shout and yell and make them laugh. He'd smack hot shots right down the rails and then he'd miss balls that a child could pocket. He'd leave a little cash behind and head to his motel for the night. The flimsy bed and the cardboard walls. The couples next door, fucking and fighting. He got so bored that he bought himself a keyboard and taught himself to play. All the tunes he loved: Elvis Presley, Bob Seger, Neil Diamond. He'd sleep late and drive around, then he'd be back in the bar pretending to drink, playing the lemon, rocking and rolling until they thought they'd got him, and then down came the hammer, out came Sneaky Pete to cut them apart. One night in a bar in Lutz, Florida, right there off State Road 597, he won $10,000 from a group of men he'd been milking for days. They came after him with a sub-machine gun, but he was gone. Gone but not forgotten, not forgotten, not Fat Rick and not Sneaky Pete.

He lived that way for a couple more years. He met a girl. She fell under his strange spell. The talk, the hair, the road, the hustle. The money in his pocket. They got married and they moved to Orlando.

It was there that he saw it first, in the bathtub of his neighbour, a vivid slick of fuming fluid.

They got talking and the guy told him all about it. He called it 'the Green'. He said it was an all-purpose removal agent, inside and out. It could clean oil from your driveway and dirt from your carpets. It was simple to make and simple to sell.

'You see,' the guy said to Rick, 'the secret is this: it's got to *look* like it works. Always remember that. And it does work.'

'Can you show me how to make it?'

With those words he was in the cleaning business for himself. Or, rather, he was in the selling business, selling cleaning fluid. He was a man of the road. He was a master salesman. He used to sell himself as a drunk pool player. Now he sold the Green, door-to-door in big plastic bottles. On the label he called it Sun-Sation, but in his mind it was always the Green.

He realised straightaway that he could never cover enough ground to get rich on his own. He formed a company, American Safety Industries. The name didn't mean anything. It didn't have to. He began recruiting crews of salesmen and teaching them how to sell it. He ran them off commission. The money flowed up the pyramid and he was at the top.

They'd find their way to him, the forgotten, the lost. He knew what they needed. Money in their pockets, dreams in their heads, Rick Parker in their hearts. He put a small ad in the paper. It said, 'DO YOU WANT TO SEE THE WORLD?' It invited them to conference rooms in downtown hotels. They weren't going to see *the* world, but they were going to see *a* world, a world that Rick Parker wanted to show them. He was looking for a particular type. He wanted street kids, he wanted them without families, he wanted them rootless and alone. He needed all of their attention, all of their time. He had a family ready for them. He gave them jobs selling Sun-Sation, he put them on the road, paid them 10 per cent of their commission every single day.

Money in their pockets. Dreams in their heads. Rick Parker in their hearts. That was how it was. That was how things worked.

The Southern states fell to him. He had crews from Florida to Los Angeles. A kid that stayed around for long enough got his own crew to run. Some of the money that flowed upwards stuck with him. More of it ran on up to Rick. The Green cost him 49 cents to make and it cost the customer $49 to buy. It was a slick operation, as slick as the Green itself.

*Imagine how it felt, shuffling in your unfamiliar chair in the function room of a chain hotel in some transit town or deadened city, your free beer warming in your lap as you watch this fat, ginger guy take to the dias in front of you and begin to talk. All of the others who've answered the same newspaper ad sit there too, doing the same as you, trying to look like they don't need what the fat man has to offer, what anyone has to offer, all of you wondering exactly what was going to happen.*

*Then he hits you like a cleaver, separating you from one world and taking you into the next.*

*'Look,' Rick Parker says, 'I started out like you. Just like you. I didn't have a watch like this one on my wrist. Didn't have a gold chain and big rings. Didn't have the Ferrari that's parked in the lot outside. But you wanna know how I got these things? You wanna know how you can get these things?'*

*He talks some more. He feels you, feels the room, takes your temperature. He waits for a certain moment, something he can weigh, a balance he can tip.*

'Hey, Denny,' he says, pointing at a kid standing to one side of the room. 'Come up here . . . This is Denny. How long you been with me, Denny?'

'Two years,' says Denny.

'How much were you making before that?'

'I didn't have a job.'

'You. Didn't. Have. A. Job?' He says each word slowly, with gaps between, like it's a sentence on its own.

'No, sir.'

'You have a place to stay?'

'I had my car.'

'You slept in your car?'

'Yes, I did.'

'What sort of car do you drive now?'

'A Pontiac. I always wanted one of those.'

'You have a home now?'

'Yes, sir, I have a home.'

'What d'you make last week?'

'Last week I made seven hundred dollars.'

'Seven. Hundred. Dollars.' Each word a sentence. 'You made seven hundred dollars. You hear that? Seven hundred dollars. Who wants to make seven hundred dollars? Quick.' The room stays still. You don't move. No one does until a kid near the front raises his hand.

'You, sir, come up here.'

The kid does.

'You want to make seven hundred dollars?'

The kid laughs.

'Sure.'

'Okay. Put your hand out. There you go.'

Rick Parker takes a wad of money from his pocket and hands it to the kid without counting it.

'That's yours, son,' he says and then turns back to the room. 'What I want to tell you is this: you can have what you want in this life, but you got to knock on the door to get it. YOU

*GOT TO KNOCK ON THE DOOR. You hear me? This man
came up and he knocked on my door while you people didn't
think to raise your hands.'*

*You shift in your seat once more, transported now, caught by
the hair and the rings, by the high Elvis voice, by the dreams
in your head and the money in his pocket.*

*'Okay,' he says, feeling the room again, feeling the new
fascination everyone has with him, his talk and his money, his
hair and his voice. 'Okay, who wants to make a hundred
dollars?'*

*This time your hand goes up. This time all the hands
around you go up, too. This time you're all listening to Rick
Parker. This time things are how he likes them.*

*'I'll guarantee you all a hundred dollars the first week you
work for me. After that it's up to you. You just got to remember
one thing: knock on the doors.'*

*'Okay, boys', you hear him say to the crew members
standing at the edges of the room, 'let's make lemonade out of
these lemons . . .'*

*And what you don't see while you have your interview with
some guy from Rick Parker's team, while you sign up and
prepare for your new life selling the green cleaner, is Fat Rick
and the kid who got the $700, laughing and joking in some
room outside as the kid gives Rick his roll of money back.*

The main lesson he taught the crews was not how to clean a
driveway or a doorstep but how to keep talking. That was the
key to selling the Green. That was the key to selling anything.
Rick learned his patter from a motivational speaker named
Zig Ziglar. Zig's was one of the names on Rick Parker's short
list of personal heroes. On it were Don King, bad Don, with his
mad bluster and his prison tricks; Elvis Presley, fat Elvis, the
hillbilly king who bought his friends and blew his money on
chimps and sandwiches, and then Zig, tiny Zig, with his
cornball philosophy and can't-fail sales systems.

He felt the sure echoes of himself bouncing back from them, in the way that the world kept coming at Don but could never quite nail him, in the way that Elvis shaped a private universe to the force of his desires; Rick knew that he was one of these new Americans, too. He was big and getting bigger. He took Zig's patter and he mixed it with his own, his fiery words between hissing breaths, his crews in thrall to his implacable will.

Rick saw the future with a piercing clarity. American Safety Industries grew. He met another girl. He left his first wife and went with the new one, and soon she bore him Chris, his first son. He met another girl, smarter than the other two, more beautiful than the other two. He paid off the second girl, took Chris and went with Holly.

Rick and Holly and Chris. He bought a place for them all down in Florida, at Daytona Beach. He bought Shar Pei dogs. He bought a long black limo. He bought jewellery and clothes. He bought the great red hair weave, the red pompadour that crowned him king. A little like Elvis with the voice and the hair. Into the business he brought his half-sister Diane, who was as smart as he was. Not many were. She made Rick money and he knew she'd never cheat him. Everyone else would, unless he watched them day and night.

He had life in his grip and this new life owed him for the lost years, his years of ginger freakdom. He bought all the women he ever wanted, gorged himself on all the blonde girls with hard bodies and flat chests who'd never looked twice at him before he became who he was. They looked at him now, he made sure of that. They looked at him in the strip clubs and in the titty bars, in the motel stops and hotel rooms. They looked into his eyes as he peeled the notes from his bankroll and slipped some their way. They looked as he laughed and did what he wanted.

By the time he was twenty-five years old, he was making $2,500 a day from selling the Green. He wore $50,000 worth of jewellery. He had a driver and bodyguards on the payroll full-time because there were people trying to steal his money and steal his business, and, anyway, he found that he hated to be alone. He wondered how far he could take it all. He looked to the other heroes on his list. He began putting on rock 'n' roll shows in Florida. He promoted the Allman Brothers. He promoted Ratt. He promoted Bon Jovi. He made money at that too, but he couldn't break right in. Then chance changed his life once more.

He found what was missing when he took a United Airlines flight from Las Vegas to Orlando and met Don King on the plane. Up there in the processed air of the thrumming tube, Rick Parker's mind boiled. Don King, his personal hero, a few rows ahead of him in the business class seats. Everyone on the plane could feel Don's presence. Rick craved eyes on him the way they lay on Don now. He swung down the aisle and took it all in: that electric hair, those hard, bright eyes so surprisingly small, the marbled teeth that lapped his mouth, the pale-brown skin on his freckled cheeks. Don's mood was good. Rick Parker amused him. Rick could hear his own high voice telling Don about the business, and how he was into rock 'n' roll now, setting up shows with the Allman Brothers and Ratt. Don said, 'Hell, son, no, that's no good, you ain't gonna get rich doing that.' He'd tried it himself and there was no money there, not real money anyhow. Too many variables, too many people to pay. What Rick needed to do was get into the boxing business instead, take his seed money and find some big white guys who could punch. Oh, he'd love it, Don said. It was like the Wild West out there, and a guy with a brain and a big white heavyweight could probably go around vacuuming up dollars off the floor. He'd do it himself if he didn't have so many other fighters to worry about.

Rick's brain howled with joy. He got off the plane and bought the Don King myth whole.

Rick Parker left Don King's head the minute he left his seat. Just another guy on another plane, somewhere in America.

Wrestlers called it kayfabe, an old word they got from the carnivals. It referred to passing off fake events as real. It was a word for the angles, feuds and gimmicks of a storyline, and for living out the storyline not just while acting it, but all of the time. Kayfabe became a way of life. It could be a way of life for a pool hustler or a cleaning salesman as much as a wrestler. Yet the true success of kayfabe came when the audience believed it too, or, even better, when they didn't know it was happening at all.

Kayfabe was about becoming. In kayfabe, good guys could become bad guys, heels could become faces, fat guys could become Elvis, nobodies could become Don King. You just had to believe in the storyline.

Fat Rick decided to do what Don King had told him to. White men, white boxers, became Rick Parker's vision, Rick Parker's dream.

# The Amazing Rocky Mundo

George Anderson returned to Chicago from Guam in the summer of 1956 to get discharged from the Coastguard. He was planning to turn around and head right back again once he was a civilian. He had a girl in Guam, and she owned a restaurant and a bar. He was going to take a job in the civil service. It would be a good life. He'd been in Guam for eighteen months with the Coastguard, and before that he'd been in Korea and before that he'd been on a weather ship that ran into a pier on Wake Island and stayed in dry dock while it was repaired. Before he joined the Coastguard he'd grown up on the South Side, the far South, been through high school there and then had two years at Western Illinois State and then another year at Northern Illinois. He loved the Coastguard and he'd almost loved the girl on Guam, but when he'd been back in Chicago for a week he knew he was done with both. He took a job with Ford aircraft for almost a year and when they shut down he drove a laundry truck for seven years and after that he joined the City of Chicago in the water department and stayed for eighteen years.

Soon after he was taken on at Ford aircraft he met Jacqueline Mundo. Her family was from the South Side, too. She was working as a dental assistant, and he called into the practice for an appointment. They were married within a year.

Tim was born in the November of '58 and his sister Erin in December of '59. It seemed like a golden time. In their family photographs they looked like the perfect nuclear unit, the handsome parents, the glowing children. Tim and Erin could sketch their early childhood in a series of idyllic scenes. They played out in winter snows, wrapped up warm against the chill of crystal winds, charging wildly into the smooth drifts and snow banks, Erin losing her boot in the dark undertow and running to the house in frozen feet, Tim laughing and shouting and clattering home behind. During green and blue summers they played baseball on shaded lawns and in open parks, Tim's arm getting stronger every day, the ball fizzing at Erin's glove. She'd catch and catch, never giving up, even when her palm burned and her fingers sang. They'd start apple and orange fights that involved the whole neighbourhood, people running and dodging everywhere, Erin and Tim at the centre of it all. That was Erin, wilful and free. And that was Tim, her guide and protector.

It appeared perfect but it wasn't. Tim had the congenital form of ileitis: the bottom part of his colon was full of ulcers and sores. Since infancy, his stomach had been tender and swollen, food passed through him, sometimes he couldn't control himself. It took a long time for the illness to be diagnosed, and when the doctors finally found out what it was they told George and Jacqueline that there was no cure. Tim needed a special diet; he could never eat sweets or junk food, I could never do what the other kids did. Because he grew up with the illness he accepted it, never questioned why he had it. He quickly learned how to hide the symptoms. He became expert at disguising the pain, absorbing it internally. On the occasions where it got the better of him, he knew which school restrooms offered him the best cover, the best opportunity to hide away.

His physical blessings were his compensation. He was good looking and athletic. Instinctively he knew how to fight, and he would. Any kid who called him names or caused him problems, he fought. Erin lost count of the times she would run home from school, her books on the sidewalk somewhere behind her, shouting, 'Mom, Tim's fighting again'. He looked out for Erin too, made sure that no one ever hurt her. All of the school knew who Tim Anderson was.

At home he hid it, too. If he'd been curled up in pain on the couch in pain, he would make sure he was standing up and running around when his father came in from work. He stuck uncomplainingly to his diet, in fact in a way he loved it. He kind of liked being different. When he had to take time out from school, Jacqueline was always there. The doctors said he couldn't play baseball or hockey or any sports, but his mother and father told him he could do anything he wanted. He and Jacqueline spent countless hours in each other's company. Her love was endless and uncomplicated. Jacqueline's father, Alex, had been a ball player, and he and George set to work on Tim. They practised for hours out in the yard and the parks. They watched all the Cubs games on TV. He was in Little League from the age of six, always the best player in the team, his arm prodigiously strong. It seemed like destiny that he would become a boy of summer, a player of America's game, a golden-haired kid with a story to tell. He got better and better. He threw perfect innings. He was the kid the other teams talked about. They all began to dream about what he might become.

George and Jacqueline had two more boys named Darrin and Tommy. They moved out of the South Side and into the suburbs, to Lansing. They had a big house in a good neighbourhood. Tim was just starting high school with a bunch of other new kids so he fitted right in. Erin had six more months of eighth grade and it was harder for her. She struggled for a while but soon she found a way. She drifted away from sports and into partying, of which Tim disapproved. He steered his own course, not a jock, not a dork, but a self-contained, straight-edge guy who didn't drink or smoke, who lived clean and took no shit. Jacqueline enrolled him in the karate school because she thought he would like the discipline of it. She was right. Soon he was kickboxing too. He loved the fight gyms from the first moment he walked in. Everything he had learned about eating the right foods, about controlling his pain, about denying his illness had a reason to it now. Here was a place where he could prove he was not weak. All of the things that had conspired against him now made him better than everyone else. He had found a way to live, and he embraced it.

They discovered that Jacqueline was ill when she and Erin went shopping for a dress for her freshman homecoming dance. They were downstairs in a big department store in the city and, as they walked upstairs, Jacqueline fainted. She was bleeding and Erin was screaming. Erin grabbed the phone, an in-house phone, and tried to dial 911. It was crazy.

It took a long time to find out what was wrong. It was a rare lung condition that became progressively worse. She began taking trips to hospital. Each time she went in, there was a chance that she might not come out, but each time she did.

Erin broke her neck in the summer of '76. She was sixteen years old, swimming in the pool at her friend's house a block from home. She dived in and hit the bottom. George was on his roof repairing the chimney when he heard the ambulance sirens. He climbed down immediately, because somehow he just knew. In the ambulance, Erin didn't think it was serious. She couldn't feel any part of her body, but she was pretty sure she'd just knocked herself out. She kept saying to the paramedics, 'Don't tell my mom, she's sick'. She didn't realise that Jacqueline was sitting right next to her.

She was in hospital for three months. Feeling returned, slowly, first to her shoulders and then to her upper arms. She thought it would just carry on coming back.

The doctors knew it wouldn't. They told Jacqueline and George that she would never walk again. They said that she would probably die before she was twenty-five.

George and Jacqueline told Erin nothing. From hospital she went to rehab in Chicago. She stayed for seven months. While she was there, she saw other patients completing their treatment and going home in wheelchairs, and she understood that this would be her fate too. When the realisation came, it was gentle, and she accepted it without complaint.

She just wanted to go home and get on with her life. The Lansing community united around her. They raised the money for the house to be adapted. The local bus drivers organised a van with a wheelchair lift so she could get around. A neighbour cooked hot meals for the family every night. George went to work, came home, saw Jacqueline and the boys then drove into Chicago to hospital to work on Erin's rehab. After three months, she came home.

Tim didn't know it had happened. He'd gone to California to stay with his grandparents, Jacqueline's mom and dad, who'd just moved out there from Chicago. Erin insisted that he wasn't told because she didn't want to spoil his trip. He knew nothing until he overheard his grandmother talking to his mother on the phone. When he got back to Lansing, he understood that Erin would live her life as a quadriplegic. He felt a tremendous tenderness towards her. He wanted to wrap his arms around her and save her from the world forever, a feeling that would never leave him. Erin had her own ideas about that. She had a boyfriend and a group of good friends and she was seventeen years old. She decided to live the same way she always had.

Jacqueline's illness became worse. She spent more time in hospital. George ran back and forwards in the same routine: work, hospital, kids. Sometimes at the end of the day, when everything was done, he would stand on the porch and stare up at the dark reefs of night cloud. Sometimes, without him knowing it, Tim would watch him, taking in all of the stillness. He felt his father's strength in these moments.

When Tim was fourteen he'd seen the Chicago Golden Gloves contest on TV and thought that he could do better than most of the fighters in it. At first he'd boxed in secret because he knew that his mother wouldn't like it and his father didn't need it and, anyway, he was going to be a baseball player not a fighter, but he came home one night with a mouse under his eye and, when Jacqueline asked, he told her all about it. She was pretty much bedridden by then, trapped at the top of the house while Erin was confined to the bottom. Tim would sneak up there after his fights and tell her about them. Sometimes, before he went out, she'd slip him some money to buy a steak dinner to build up his strength. He grew into an athlete's life. He didn't have to articulate to Jacqueline why he did it; she understood.

He learned how to fight while his stomach was bad. He learned how to control his bowels when food was running right through him and some other guy was punching him in the guts. He learned that his will was stronger than his body, and if he made his will strong enough he could overcome anything.

He needed a ring name to enter on the competition lists, so he called himself Rocky Mundo in honour of the *Rocky* movies and Jacqueline's maiden name. It made her laugh when he finally told her.

She died soon after Erin graduated high school. If Tim had been a writer, he might have got a novel out of it, one of those slim and aching volumes from creative writing MAs. But he wasn't. He was a fighter. He fought in Jacqueline's name and with her name. He fought to honour her and to avenge her fate. He felt she was with him when he did. By the time he went away to college to play baseball, he'd fought more than a hundred and fifty times and lost no more than a handful.

It was obvious, too, that he was more than just a college ball player. He was blowing kids away with the strength of his arm. The Chicago Cubs took him on and sent him down to Boca Raton to pitch for one of their farm teams in the AAA leagues.

He needed to make extra money so he signed up as a doorman at a club called Summers On The Beach in Fort Lauderdale. Summers was a big place. Five or six hundred people a night showed up there. He loved it and everyone loved him. Girls flocked to him. He was a good bouncer, stern and calm, strong when he needed to be. He became friends with a couple of other doormen, Kevin Finn, who wanted to be a football player, and Jim Murphy, who was getting into the medical legal business. Jim was looking out for room-mates and soon Tim moved in.

The major leagues slipped away from him season by season. He was a fine pitcher. He threw curves and sliders and change-ups and they were as good as anyone's. But his fastball wasn't fast enough. In the minor leagues you could blow by guys throwing at eighty-five or eighty-six miles per hour. In the majors it was three or four miles per hour short. The hitters there had hand–eye coordination from the gods. The extra fraction of a second that Tim's fastball took to reach the plate opened up a whole world to them.

He could have gone on pitching in the minor leagues. The Cubs wanted him to. But he was still fighting so they offered an ultimatum: either pitch or box. He thought about being thirty years old and throwing old-man sliders at blond-haired kids arriving from the big city, telling them how he might once have made the big show. He let baseball go.

He was taken on by a boxing trainer named Augie
Rodriguez. Augie had a gym in Drew Park, on Anderson
Road. He used a matchmaker named Pete Susens, from
Indiana. Through Augie and Pete, Tim made his pro debut on
14 June 1983 at the Sherwood Club in Indianapolis. He
outpointed Floyd Saunders over four rounds. He was twenty-
four years old and weighed 174? pounds. In July he
outpointed John Cox at the Americana Congress Hotel in
Chicago and in September he outpointed Floyd Saunders
again in Hammond, Indiana, and James Wilder in Milwaukee,
Wisconsin. In November he went back to Milwaukee and got
outpointed by James Wilder in a narrow decision, and seven
days later he returned to Hammond, Indiana, and registered
his first professional knockout, in round number one of his
fight with Steve Cooper. Over the next thirty months, he beat
Jim Hearn, Pedro Garcia, David Carter and Donald Myert; he
beat James Angel, Louis Pappin and Frank Lux twice, and he
also lost to Frank Minton and Bob Smith. He fought in
Indiana, Chicago and Las Vegas. He went from four-rounders
to ten-rounders, he went from 174? to 199 pounds, he went
from novice to professional, he went from pitcher to boxer.

He began to wonder how much moore Augie and Pete
could do for him. Pete sent him to Paris, France, to fight
Angelo Mussone. He lost in two rounds. He flew home and
split for California.

This was how it happened. His fastball wasn't fast enough
and he was white and he could fight. He still loved baseball
and he thought about it often. He remembered how it felt to
throw the curves and sliders, to watch them arc from his hand
towards the plate. He remembered the sound they made as
they cleaved the air, he remembered the thousands of balls he
threw at Erin and at George and at Alex Mundo. He thought
of his mother, his Jacqueline. He thought of Erin, now at
college, in her chair but as free as she ever was, and he

thought of George back home in Chicago, out on the porch as night fell and the rain came down from the banked blue clouds, the streetlights shining in the wet stone of the sidewalk in front of the house.

# The Worst Man You Never Knew

Fat Rick met the man who would kill him in LA. What brought them together depended on what you believed in: fate, luck, kismet, destiny. Rick didn't give a fuck about any of that. He'd have put it down to dumb chance, to a directionless and hostile universe if he'd known about it but he didn't feel a thing when he shook hands with Tim Anderson for the first time, no hint, no tremor. It was the summer of 1986. Tim had just been to France, to Paris, to fight a guy called Angelo Mussone. In round number two, Mussone had brushed him with a glove and the ref jumped in and stopped the fight. That's how things went in France. It was a long way to go for two rounds. Tim got back home, split with his trainer, and came out to California to stay with his grandparents and spar at a gym called Benny The Jet's.

They met in a hotel out by the airport on a Sunday night. A musician called Doug Wilder hooked them up. Doug knew Rick from a gig he'd played with the Allman Brothers. Doug knew Tim because he worked out at Benny The Jet's.

Doug knew that Rick was looking for a way into the boxing business. Doug drove Tim out there. They parked up and walked into the bar. It was jammed with people. The noise was tremendous. They were shouting to be heard above each other. They were all kids, slightly too excited to appear comfortable, too poorly dressed and wild to look like they belonged. In the far corner of the room, Rick Parker was playing the piano and singing, loudly. He had a crowd around him, clapping and cheering.

'Uh-huh-huh,' he sang. 'Oh yeah . . . Oh yeah . . .'

'Is that him?' Tim asked.

'That's him,' Doug said. 'That's Rick. Come and say hi.'

A half-hour later, they sat down to dinner. Tim took Rick in for the first time. The blue bomber jacket and the open-neck shirt. The big gold rings and the Elvis shades. The cool Southern charm and the warm Southern voice. He seemed to swallow up the noise around him.

He talked and talked. He told Tim about the bands he'd promoted, talked about the cleaning crews and the Green. He spoke about the day that had changed his life, meeting Don King on an aeroplane flight. Hearing Don talk about the boxing game. Taking Don's advice on what to do next.

Rick said, 'I like you, Tim. This is what I'd like you to do. You introduce me to some people. I'll get you the fights and I'll promote them myself. I'll pay you $750 a week, I'll give you half of the money from your fights and after it gets going pretty good, you and I will get a percentage of the promotional rights.'

Tim didn't need long to weigh it up. What could he lose? It was over with Augie. He wasn't quite sure where his life was going.

'I need you to fight at heavyweight,' Rick said. 'The heavyweight division is where the money is. It's like Don King told me: if you can find a white guy who can fight for the heavyweight championship, then you got millions and millions of dollars right there in one night. I call it the windfall factor. Millions and millions, all at one time. That's what I'm meaning to do. That's what we can do together.'

Tim told Rick it would take him six months to bulk up enough to fight as a heavyweight. He would do it the right way, no steroids or any of that junk. He'd train hard and eat well. He'd put on fifteen pounds of lean muscle. In the meantime, he'd introduce Rick to some people. He could open doors for Rick Parker, doors into the boxing business. By the time they'd finished the meal, they were together.

The world Fat Rick wanted into was the world of Don King. Don King. What a motherfucker Don King was. 'Only In America' was Don's favourite saying. And no wonder. Only in America could someone like Don King get away with the kind of stuff Don King liked to get away with. Within Don lay the history of modern boxing. He was born in Cleveland, Ohio, where he ran a numbers game, walking around with a loaded Magnum in his belt and thousands of dollars in a roll in his pocket. It was 1966. He dressed like a pimp and talked like a preacher. His nickname was 'Donald The Kid'. The get-up and the bluster disguised a brilliant mind. He had already killed a man. It had happened twelve years before. Hillary Brown was a stick-up artist who tried to rob Donald The Kid's gambling house. Hillary the stick-up man pulled his gun and Donald The Kid pulled his, and, at the end of it, Hillary Brown was dead. The county prosecutor called it justifiable homicide. For one time only, Donald The Kid found himself in wholehearted agreement with the justice system.

But Don was a street genius. His numbers game was a beautiful kind of lottery. Every day poor people bet on a three-digit number. The winning number was the three digits in the middle column of the final daily market stock quotations. Each day at 2 p.m. Don called a broker in New York.

Based on the broker's estimates, he could work out more accurately what the final number might be. Then he could place thirty or forty bets on the various digit combinations he worked out in his head, and quite often hit the number. His $1 bets paid out at 500-1. Don was making $15,000 a day from his own bets and from taking other people's.

He'd taken a bet from an old friend of his called Sam Garrett. Sam didn't know that Don called a stockbroker every day at 2 p.m. He didn't know that Don was some kind of maths phenom. He didn't know any of it. Sam just liked to bet on the numbers. He had TB and one kidney and he wanted a quiet life. Now he owed Donald The Kid $600. Don found him and stomped him to death while a crowd of people watched. The cops showed up in time to hear Sam Garrett's last words. As he lay in the gutter at the corner of Cedar Street and East 100, he said, 'I'll pay you the money, Don'. The detectives had trouble getting the cuffs around Don King's thick wrists. Sam Garrett lay in the hospital for five days. Doctors put his chances of survival at 500-1. Sam never was much good at beating those odds. Donald The Kid was charged with murder in the second degree and found guilty. He should have got life, but the Judge, Hugh Corrigan, suspended the sentence pending appeal. Don served three years and eleven months for stomping Sam. While he was in prison, on the radio he listened to Joe Frazier fight Muhammad Ali for the first time. When they fought for the third time, five years later, Don King, no longer Donald The Kid, was the promoter. That fight, the Thrilla In Manila, became one of the two best-known fights in the post-war history of boxing. The other, the Rumble In The Jungle between Muhammad Ali and George Foreman, was also promoted by Don. In the process he outnegotiated religious leaders and African despots. He became as famous as the guys who were fighting, and richer, too.

When Judge Hugh Corrigan ran for appointment to the

Court of Appeals in 1976, Muhammad Ali campaigned for him.

Don's killing spree ended at two, unless you included financial killings. He made plenty more of those. He stuck with Ali, took the cash, went with Larry Holmes after that, and then a few years of nearly men and lost boys like Tim Witherspoon and Pinklon Thomas until he wrestled a kid named Mike Tyson away from a decent man called Bill Cayton and took more money with Mike than anyone ever thought could be made in boxing.

Rick projected his fantasies of wealth and fame on to Don. He saw himself reflected back in the sharp glare of Don's brilliance. Hadn't he had his first taste of money down on the streets? Didn't he understand the electric charge of a gun and a roll of cash? Couldn't he talk as fast and look as memorable?

Don was the alpha and omega of American boxing. And the cut that Don didn't have for himself, Bob Arum did. While Don had been running numbers and doing time, Bob was at Harvard Law School, working as a taxation expert on Wall Street, for the DA's office in New York and then in the Justice Department for the Kennedy administration. He'd never stomped any of his enemies and he didn't have a nickname like 'Robert The Kid'. He was not a street genius, but a very clever man who thought that boxing was just two guys clubbing each other over the head. The closest he'd come to the fight game was at the Justice Department in New York when he'd headed the taxation department that investigated the first fight between Floyd Patterson and Sonny Liston. Sonny had come to the office asking for his money.

Ten years later, Sonny was dead and Bob was in boxing. He and Don filled the power vacuum left by the mob. Don had the heavyweights sewn up so Bob made middleweight superfights like Hagler versus Hearns and Leonard versus Duran. Boxing proved the ultimate democracy. It was run by a numbers guy and a Harvard graduate. It was run not on fine business principles nor with the rat-cunning of the street savant. It was run on force of personality. It was run on the principle that the promoter was always going to be the fucking bad guy. Rick Parker accepted those facts into his heart. He wanted the pie, not the crumbs. He bought the Don King myth wholesale. He was in. Rick Parker was in.

It was the early spring of '87. Fat Rick took his limo from Phoenix, Arizona, to LA. In the car with him were Tim Anderson, Joe Derrick and Randall 'Tex' Cobb. Tex was one of the toughest white guys in America. He'd been in a fight with Larry Holmes for the Heavyweight Championship of the World that was so brutal and one-sided, Holmes had won every one of the fifteen rounds, yet he couldn't knock Tex Cobb down, couldn't put a dent in him. Tex had one of the greatest chins of all time. Larry might as well have been punching the ring post. Tex became a hero after that night, with his car-crash face and unbroken will. He fought on. He won sometimes and he lost sometimes, and the crowds loved him either way. He had a tremendous store of one-liners for any occasion. When someone asked if he'd consider a rematch with Holmes, he said he didn't think that Larry's hands could take it. He began a second career in movies playing characters he described as 'extremely hairy, expressionless tough guys'.

Tex liked being in the movies, but he still wanted to box, too. He hadn't had a fight in almost a year and a half. He'd lost his last four and he was out of proper shape, but he was as tough as ever inside. He was too good to be an opponent, but no longer a contender. He needed to start again. That was a problem for Joe Derrick to solve. Joe was Tex's manager and the other passenger in the car. He looked more like a jock than a boxing manager. He liked to work out. He had a condo in Manhattan Beach and a hope that Tex Cobb was his ticket out. As he rode back home in Rick Parker's limo, he thought maybe their time had come.

*White men, white boxers become Rick's vision, Rick's dream.*

*He names his dream The Windfall Factor: millions and millions of dollars, all at one time, all in one night. These visions obsess him. Fat Rick does what Don King told him to do. He dips his toe into the boxing business. Tim goes to live with Joe Derrick in the condo at the beach. Tim becomes Tex Cobb's training partner. Tim tells Rick that Tex can still fight. Tim tells Rick some funny stuff about Joe; about coming home to the condo to find a girl tied up and left there . . . Rick smiles. Rick laughs. Rick understands Joe better than Tim ever will.*

*Joe gets Rick into cocaine. Cocaine rocks Fat Rick's world like nothing else. He's dabbled before, but it wasn't like this, it wasn't like Joe's magic supply. Joe's supply galvanises his ambition, solidifies his vision, enhances his gifts. Now he under-stands absolutely what is possible, what he is capable of, what he has become. 'This,' he thinks, 'is how Don King must feel'.*

*Rick takes Tim to Springfield, Missouri, for his heavyweight debut. Springfield, Missouri, is where Rick Parker was born. Tim fights a guy named Frank Lux, who he's already beaten twice as a cruiserweight. Frank Lux appears under the alias Frank Williams. Frank catches Tim Anderson cold and knocks him out in round number two. Rick doesn't care. No one is there to see it.*

*In his marrow, in his bones, the feeling.*

*He dreams his dream of a white champion, of the windfall factor.*

*White men, white boxers. Rick Parker, their fat white king.*

Sharon Hodge knew she was going to marry Tex Cobb the first day she met him. It was the summer of '82. She was a DJ on a morning show in El Paso, Texas. She'd only had Tex on the programme as a favour to a friend who liked boxing. She didn't. She saw right through it. He asked her out for a breakfast that went on and on right through the day. Tex thrummed with life and good humour, a classic high-IQ tough guy, rare as a snow leopard. They were together for a while and then Tex went off and married someone else. Sharon still knew. Late in '85, she was watching *The Tonight Show* on TV, and there was Tex. She remembered that *The Tonight Show* always put its guests in the Sheraton Universal, so she called. They put her through to his room. Some other boxer answered and he put Tex on the line.

The strange thing was, it turned out that *The Tonight Show* was a rerun. Tex wasn't in town for the programme at all, he'd just come to meet his friend. The girl on the front desk had seen him walk in. Fate, luck, kismet. Easy.

Sharon saw through Joe Derrick right away. He was stealing Tex's money. Tex was so stubborn he wouldn't hear it, from her or from anyone. She took one look at Fat Rick with his ginger quiff and his Elvis shades and laughed out loud. She'd interviewed Presley in the last year of his life. The King had invited her to his hotel room. She knew a fake when she saw one. Tim Anderson was the only one she liked, the only good guy she could see, funny and gentle and kind.

Her and Tim, in with the wrong people, here in this great wrong place.

Rick and Joe came up with a plan to put Tex back in the big money. They'd go on a tour, nine fights in three months, club shows against club fighters with Tex getting in shape and building his record. They hit the road; Tex and Sharon, Fat Rick and Tim Anderson, Rick's sister Diane, and a rolling cast of cleaning crew kids and Rick's bodyguards. They began in Hot Springs, Arkansas, on 12 March. Tex knocked out Phil Rendine in round number two and Tim knocked out Juan Pablo Rodriguez in round number five. On 21 March they arrived in Springfield, Missouri, where Tex knocked out Frank Williams, who was really Frank Lux fighting under another of his aliases, in round number two and Tim knocked out Dave Carrington in round number four. They went to Fayetteville, Arkansas, on 26 March, where Tex knocked out Stan Johnson in round number one and Tim outpointed Bobby Ellis after round number eight. On 31 March they were in Richmond, Kentucky, where Tex knocked out Frankie Albert, who was really Frank Lux, in round number one, and Tim didn't fight. They went to Terre Haute, Indiana, on 6 April, where Tex knocked out Louis Pappin in round number one and Tim didn't fight. The following night, in Lincoln, Nebraska, Tex knocked out Rick Kellar in round number two and Tim didn't fight. Ten days after that, on 17 April in Springfield, Mississippi, Tex had a one-round draw with Bill Duncan when Bill had to pull out after an accidental clash of heads, and Tim knocked out Jesse Brown in round number two. They went to Daytona Beach, Florida, on 11 May where Tex knocked out Aaron Brown in round number five and Tim knocked out Larry Somerset in round number four. They finished up in Birmingham, Alabama, on 29 May, where Tex knocked out Michael Johnson in round number six and Tim got outpointed by John Barbier after round number eight.

Tex's record went from 25-7 to 33-7-1. He didn't fight anyone good enough to beat him. He couldn't have survived nine fights in three months if he had. He fought against club fighters, against barroom tough guys and bouncers and journeymen. He fought the kind of fighters they portrayed in B-movies, the kind that got called tomato cans and palookas, in the shorthand of boxing writers.

Everywhere they went was a party. Sharon loathed it. Rick's cleaning cash was floating the tour. He threw his money around on cocaine and strippers. Every night they weren't boxing, Rick was in the nearest titty bar handing dollars to the girls, paying them more to come back to his hotel room and party. They careened through the South, stopping for a few days here, a week or so there. Tim was the only one who trained seriously. Sharon sometimes wondered what he was doing in boxing.

She stayed on tour for Tex. He was still full of his tough-guy charm. Sharon sheltered in his slipstream. They lurched into Florida for their final few days.

They went to Rick's place in Daytona Beach, near Highway 95 in Pelican Bay. It was set down by the water in a quiet part of town. Not even a whisper of the highway. Other large houses stood on either side, lent distance by money. Sprinklers turned on the green grass. Under blue skies, under golden suns, in celestial light, the big white houses glowed. Rick had the limo and the sports car on the drive, a pool table and a bar in the den, a deck under the cool of the trees at the water's edge. They stayed a week or so. Tex's divorce became final on 4 May and he and Sharon got married the very next day at the house. Rick took care of everything. He insisted. He paid for it all, found the minister and laid on the party. He even bought Tex's wedding band. Rick and Joe were the official witnesses. No family, no friends, just her and Tex, Fat Rick and Holly, Joe, Tim, Rick's driver Stuart and Doug Wilder with his guitar. Just another day on tour. They married in the house and took drinks out on the deck that overlooked the water. Many years later, when everything was over, Sharon Cobb would look back at the names of the two dead men on her wedding certificate and realise that it was haunted by ghosts from the start.

Joe Derrick killed himself on Independence Day, 1987. He did it at the condo in Manhattan Beach. He put a shotgun in his mouth. The shells took the top of his head clean off. Tim found his body. He knew that there was something wrong almost as soon as he got the door open, a sense of stillness, the stillness and then the smell, the smell of copper and iron so strong it hit the back of his tongue. He could taste it as well as smell it. Joe was on his knees on the living room floor. His blood was falling from the popcorn ceiling back down on to him. His brains lay at his feet. In front of him was the shotgun. He'd come to rest with his back to the wall, his head hanging forwards. Tim walked quickly around the room. He went to the kitchen to see if anyone was there. The place was empty. He could hear fireworks exploding at the beach.

Tim and Rick went to the funeral. Tex was in Detroit with Sharon making a film called *Collision Course* with Jay Leno. Rick rang to tell them the news. Tim left the condo the night he found Joe and never went back.

*Fat Rick drives to the condo in Manhattan Beach. He pulls up in the driveway and kills the engine. He turns out the headlights. It's 3 a.m. He hears the sea winds blowing in, whistling past the curves of his car. On crystalline sinuses, a brittle cocaine high. The last of the rush he has come to love. Joe's parting gift to him, a drug he was born to adore. He settles back in his seat and breathes in.*

*Goodbye Joe, you stupid fuck. What did you want to do that for?*

*He opens the silver case on the passenger seat. He takes out his tiny silver gun. He slips his finger through the trigger guard. He points the gun at his temple. He laughs to himself.*

*Nah, he's not that kind of guy. Not like Joe.*

*Rick thinks about weakness. He thinks about pain. He understands their currency, he feels all the weakness of the world. Weakness he does not have.*

*He replaces the gun inside his case. The silver locks click shut. He throws his car into gear and drives back to his hotel room, away from Joe Derrick and towards his future with Randall 'Tex' Cobb.*

# An Interlude: What Bugs Tim About Rick

*B*ack *when he was first working as a bodyguard for Rick, something had happened. It wasn't long after he'd first taken the job. He was hanging out with Rick all the time. Rick could never be alone. He wanted Tim to get him in shape, so they swam together and played racketball every day. Rick had a natural eye for a ball, nothing like Tim's, but not bad. Rick would encourage Tim to wear more outrageous clothes, to dress like a wrestler or a rock star. He liked the way women flocked around Tim when he did. Tim met Rick's sister Diane. He liked her right away. He met the other men who worked for Rick; his English driver, Stuart. His bodyguards and crew managers.*

*Rick had asked Tim to do something for him, take care of a crew kid who was causing him problems, dealing drugs. Tim could show him up, sort him out, teach him right from wrong. Hit him a few times in front of everyone else. Humiliate him like he was humiliating Rick. They could do it on a Sunday night, when Rick called everyone together at the hotel. Tim said nothing and hoped Rick would forget it.*

*Sunday night at the hotel, everyone was drinking and laughing. Suddenly, there was Fat Rick before them, all crazed and wired, making one of his big entrances. He did his usual thing, whipping them up. Then he said: 'There's someone here we need to speak to. There's someone here who is causing us harm.'*

*He pulled the kid from the swarm in front of him. The kid looked afraid.*

*'You know what he's been doing, don't you,' Rick said.*

*The kid was all panic. He looked around and saw the door. He pushed through it and ran outside into the car park. Rick went after him, followed by the rest.*

*They came together in the car park, away from the buildings at its farthest end, away from the last of the vehicles left at its edges. It was quiet. They cast long shadows in the sodium flare of the security lights. The night hummed. They formed a circle around Rick and the kid.*

*Rick said to Tim, 'I want you to hit this kid hard.'*

*Tim refused. Some of the other crew kids began to shout at him, telling him to do it, like Rick said. Tim stared them down. Moments passed. Tim thought that might be it, but Rick wasn't done.*

*One of Rick's guys put his arm behind his back and pulled a short-barrelled gun from under his jacket. He took a few steps forward. He was in the middle of the circle, in front of the kid.*

*'Open your mouth,' he said.*

*The kid's eyes opened wide, but nothing else did. The guy put the gun in his face.*

*'Open it,' he said again. The kid did this time, more in surprise than anything else, and as he did the guy's arm extended, punch-fast. The gun went in and came out. It made no sound. The kid fell backwards very quickly. Blood began to flow from between his teeth. He didn't move at all.*

*For a moment, no one said anything. Tim stood at the back of the group. To him it felt like the oxygen void in the seconds after lightning in an electrical storm, that sharp, hot vacuum. Fat Rick reacted first.*

*'Get out of here,' he said. 'Meet at the Holiday Inn in one hour. Drive different ways.'*

*They fanned out and headed for their cars. Tim, in shadow, watched them go. He looked back at the kid, who lay on his back with one knee drawn up. His head was to one side. He was a dark shape on the dark ground. Thick black blood had spread from his mouth across the concrete. It had soaked his shirtfront. He was as still as everything around him: the few parked cars, the buildings in relief against the massed sky.*

*Tim thought: 'He's dead. He must be dead.' He couldn't believe it had happened. He waited a few more minutes while his head cleared and then he ran out of the car lot and across the road to an all-night store. He picked up the payphone. He dialled 911 and spoke to the police. He told them there was a body in the car lot across the street. He hung up. There was nothing more he could do. When he came back out of the store, he could still see the shape, low to the ground. He found his car. It was the moment that he should have left, but he didn't.*

*The next day he was in the gym early, hitting the heavy bag, letting it all go. He wished he'd hit the kid. He wished he'd hit the kid when Rick had told him to. Then the kid would have got a broken nose and that would have been all. Now there was this.*

*Then there was the whole thing with Joe Derrick. Finding the body was bad enough. The sight and the smell he could never forget. It had been the Fourth of July. There were fireworks down on Manhattan Beach after dark. He and Joe were planning to go. In the morning, they worked out together as usual and then Joe went and got a haircut and a manicure. They arranged to meet back at the apartment. And they had, after a fashion . . .*

*Tim brooded on Joe's death. He tried to reconcile what he saw with what he knew about Joe. Sometimes, his mind ran obsessive circuits, looking for explanations:*

*– Joe's divorced and in debt. Joe's hooked on drugs. He is receiving threats about the money he owes – $70k to some heavy people. He knows that Rick Parker wants Tex Cobb. He has a sudden suicidal impulse and he shoots himself in the head.*

*– Joe has been thinking about it for months, no, for years. The day will come, and when it does he will know. He feels it as soon as he wakes. He puts his plan into operation. He does all of the things he likes one more time. He lifts weights. He has his hair and nails done. He spends the day at the beach and then goes home and blows his brains out.*

*– Joe comes home to find two men he does not want to see in his apartment. They force him to the floor and put the rifle in his mouth. They tell him he can have it the easy way or the hard way, but either way, he's getting it. He pulls the trigger before they do something worse.*

*Round and round they go, the blood in a car park and blood on a ceiling, these things about Rick that are bugging Tim Anderson.*

# 178,000 Reasons

*N*ovember 1987. Fat Rick stood in all of his trash finery
in a temporary outdoor gym at the Enclave Beach Club in
Orlando, the great red pompadour glowing under the winter
sun. He was watching a boxer move around the ring. Joe
Derrick had been dead for four months. Tex Cobb had a new
manager, a guy named Ron Weathers. Ron was the reason
Rick was here. The man Fat Rick had come to see was
thirty-eight years old, 260 pounds, as big as a rhino and as
unfathomably strong. He moved slowly, but with purpose.
His name was George Foreman, former heavyweight
champion of the world. He was making a comeback after
ten years out of boxing. Rick Parker was his new promoter.
Fat Rick strutted around for a while between the journalists
and radio people and fans and sightseers before taking up
a position just below the bottom rope. George didn't see
him, didn't see anyone. He just kept swinging heavy
punches one arm at a time until his big bald head was awash
with sweat, and then he called for a towel and stood with
his huge arms over the top rope, chatting and laughing with
the people in the crowd.

Everyone in boxing thought the comeback was a joke, but Rick Parker knew it wasn't. He'd understood it right away. George said he was fighting to pay for a youth centre at his church in Texas, and maybe he was. The new George was a different George from the angry and fragile kid who could not survive the destruction of his ego down by the banks of the Congo at Don King's Rumble In The Jungle. The new George was an affable man of God, spreading good vibes. But Rick watched those heavy punches going in, one after the other, and he knew that George still had the dark fighting place in his heart and needed to give it expression. Rick felt it, even if no one else did.

George's return had begun in Sacramento, California back in March against a journeyman named Steve Zouski. Steve's record was 25-11. He'd lost ten of his last fourteen. Mike Tyson had just rerouted his nose at the Nassau Coliseum. Who knew how much Big George really weighed in that ring – he said it was 267 pounds, but it might have been anything. His shorts began right under his chest. Zouski was tough, but George knocked him out at the end of round number four. Four months to the day after the Zouski fight, he'd knocked out Charles Hostetter in round number three at the Oakland Coliseum and two months after that he knocked out Bobby Crabtree in round number six in Springfield, Missouri. He was twenty pounds lighter already. The comeback still meant nothing to anyone in boxing, but Rick Parker knew.

Big George found God after having a near-death experience. He'd come back a year after the loss to Ali in '74, and he'd beaten Ron Lyle and Joe Frazier, Scott LeDoux, John Dino Denis and Pedro Agosto. Then he went to San Juan and lost on points to Jimmy Young. In the dressing room afterwards, semi-conscious from exhaustion and heatstroke, he found himself in 'a hellish place of nothingness and despair'. He begged God to help him and promised to change his ways. He stopped boxing that night and became the ordained minister of a church in Houston. He told people that Jimmy Young had knocked the devil out of him.

*Ron Weathers is Rick Parker's lightning rod. He's a serious man, not like Joe Derrick. He has interests in more than one fighter. When George Foreman wants to make a comeback, Ron takes a piece of it. Ron brings in Fat Rick. Fat Rick brings money and a monomaniacal belief in George Foreman.*

*After Big George kayos Bobby Crabtree in his third comeback fight, Fat Rick speaks to the press. He tells them: 'It's a treacherous business, real treacherous. In this business you're always watching your back. But I love it. This business teaches you how to succeed against all odds, how to keep going when all sorts of obstacles are in your way.*

*'In boxing,' Rick Parker says, 'the show is as important as the business, and Don King and Bob Arum and all of them had better watch out, because if Rick Parker ever gets TV, they're in trouble. I could get any fighter in the world . . .'*

*And as he speaks these words, he knows them to be true.*

The comeback stood at 3 and 0. It still meant nothing to the world of boxing, nothing to Bob Arum and nothing to Don King, nothing to twenty-one-year-old Mike Tyson, the undefeated, undisputed heavyweight champion of the world, just about to knock out Tyrell Biggs and Larry Holmes and scale his awesome peak. George Foreman was old and he was slow. He was fat and he was fucked. But he had Ron Weathers and he had Rick Parker. To them, it lived.

*Tex Cobb tells Fat Rick about a guy he met after his fight with Aaron Brown at Finkies in Daytona, a good guy by the name of Doug Davis. Doug owns a bar just up the coast from Daytona in Ormond Beach. Turns out that he might be* *interested in tasting a little excitement, making a little money. Rick calls Doug for the first time from Houston, Texas, a week or so later. He keeps calling and he keeps talking. He can feel the yearning, he can sense the wish for a better life. The salesman's gift. The hustler's instinct. Slowly, skilfully, he floats the idea of Doug Davis buying a 10 per cent share in the comeback of George Foreman for $50,000.*

*Doug thinks about it, weighs it up. Fifty is a lot of money for a guy with a bar business and a home and two young sons. He talks about it with his wife. He feels the pull of boxing. He throws the dice. They sign a note of agreement on an October afternoon in Doug's bar. Fat Rick gets his fat hands on Doug's money a few days later. Doug gets a 10 per cent stake in a company called Sports Day Inc., a company newly formed by Richard L. Parker for the purpose, as specified in the note of agreement, of 'providing professional boxing, promotions, entertainment, management of sports personalities and especially the boxing careers of: Randall "Tex" Cobb, Tim "Doc" Anderson, George Foreman, Frank "Gator" Lux, Tony Perea, Irish Dan Murphy, Angel "Fatso" Madino, David Acosta, Victoria Belcher and Eddie Reos and other sports personalities and including television, movies and other profit making promotions'.*

*Rick Parker sells Doug Davis a dream, a simple variation of the dreams he sells to everyone: dreams of a cleaner house, dreams of a better job, dreams of an easier life. If the deal was one for liquor supplies or security contracts or property purchase, perhaps Doug sees its flaws, keeps away. But it isn't and he doesn't. This isn't normal life. It is boxing and it is different.*

Tim Anderson put his doubts about Fat Rick aside when Rick told him he could fight George Foreman in Orlando. Tim was sure he could win. It would be Sports Day Inc.'s first event. They hired a kid called Randy Gerber to drum

up the press. Randy was doing PR for the Enclave Beach
Club on International Drive, just across the road from Wet
N Wild. The Enclave put up a ring in the car park. Tim and
George began to hang out there. They held open training
sessions at 3 p.m. The press and radio guys came down
almost every day. They loved Tim Anderson. He dyed his
hair even blonder and had a spiky cut, just like Sting. He
travelled around with a busful of girls called the Beverly
Hills Knockouts whom he knew from Summers On The
Beach. Everywhere Tim went to promote the fight, the
Knockouts went too, all over Orlando in a big yellow coach
with 'TIM "DOC" ANDERSON AND THE BEVERLY
HILLS KNOCKOUTS' painted in red letters on the sides.
The Knockouts wore red bomber jackets and white stiletto
heels and cut-down T-shirts that skimmed their navels. Tim
stood around like a god, honed and taut.

George Foreman watched on with amusement. He remembered with a smile when he was that young and fit. He liked
Tim; he couldn't help it. There was something about the guy.
He was free and happy and doing what he loved. George was
a contented man, too. He was kind and softly spoken and he
laughed a lot. The good vibes spread. Tex Cobb showed up
and told more jokes and funny stories. The mood was
infectious. Randy Gerber held a contest to find the ring card
girls. He ended up at the mansion of Michael Peters.
Michael lived there surrounded by women who danced in a
nightclub he owned called the Doll House. The women wore
very little, sometimes nothing. Michael told Randy to take
his pick.

'Hell, they'll walk round the ring naked if you want 'em
to.'

Randy laughed. He struck a deal with Michael Peters for
the Doll House to sponsor the fight. Michael took Randy and
Tim to dinner with ten of the girls to celebrate. They all sat
around wondering how much better life could get.

**Orlando Sentinel**, 15 November 1987, section C-18
Area Answers Bell With Foreman Fight
**By Brian Schmitz**

Professional boxing is back to stay in Orlando – or at least as long as Greg Hoenig's bank account holds out . . .

Hoenig found his old friend Rick Parker to promote boxing's return to Orlando. With his red beard, tinted glasses and collection of jewellery, Parker looks more like a rock 'n' roll promoter – because he is. Putting on shows for Ratt, Bon Jovi, the Marshall Tucker Band and Jason and the Scorchers was exciting for Parker. But he wanted to manage a heavyweight champion. 'I wanted to get the next great white hope,' said Parker.

He wound up with Anderson, who was a friend of a singer Parker once promoted. Parker had Anderson appear on the undercard of Tex Cobb's comeback tour. Cobb is managed by Ron Weathers, who also manages George Foreman and is a friend of New York matchmaker Bruce Trampler. Trampler used to make matches in Orlando for Pete Ashlock. Maybe now you're beginning to figure out how Foreman–Anderson ended up at that old barn-like stadium in East Orlando.

*Randy Gerber goes to meet Rick Parker at the Sheraton Twin Towers in Orlando to update him on the last of the PR for the fight. Fat Rick is up in his room with four or five other guys, only a couple of whom Randy recognises. On the coffee table between them sits Rick Parker's silver gun. Randy has never seen a gun before in his life. It scares him shitless. Rick watches him looking at it.*

*'Okay, Randy, what's happening?' he says.*

*Randy gives his PR report. When he's finished he and Rick look down at the gun.*

*'Thanks, Randy,' says Fat Rick. 'You can fuck off now.'*

*The men around the table laugh. Randy hears them as he leaves.*

*Tim Anderson fights George Foreman on 21 November 1987 at the Eddie Graham Sports Complex in Orlando. Traffic is backed up as far as Highway 50. Outside the arena it's like a Hollywood movie première. Klieg lights fly over the heads of the crowd as they walk towards the doors. The bus full of Beverly Hills Knockouts pulls up to cheers. Every seat in the Eddie Graham Sports Complex has been sold. The fight will be broadcast live throughout Florida. Tim shadowboxes in his dressing room to keep down his nerves. For the last few days, food has been going right through him. Nerves and his stomach condition. The undercard fights pass like hearses, slow and filled with dread. The Beverly Hills Knockouts walk with him to the ring. The PA plays 'Ridin' The Storm Out' by REO Speedwagon. Tim steps through the ropes and waits. George Foreman enters wearing a black robe over the top of a red robe. When he pulls down his hood, steam rises from his shaved head. The Beverly Hills Knockouts stand on the ring apron in a line. A couple of the girls shuffle to Tim's corner. They kiss him and ruffle his hair. Tim smiles.*

*Fat Rick is the night's MC. Black tuxedo and a red cummerbund. Clean white shirt and a red bow tie. Elvis shades and shiny shoes. The great red hairpiece on his head. A microphone in his fat right hand.*

*He introduces the fighters. Doug Wilder sings 'The Star Spangled Banner'. George is still in his big black robe. He puts his right hand over his heart as he listens to the anthem. Tim strips down to black shorts with a white side stripe, black boots and long white socks. He jogs on the spot and looks around.*

The lights and the girls and the steam rising from George Foreman's shaven head.

His dad and his sister watch from ringside. Erin looks at George and smiles.

George Foreman removes his robes. More steam rises from his body. He outweighs Tim by fifty pounds. He wears his big white shorts pulled right up over his stomach.

Tim is winning round number one until the last ten seconds when George hits him with a single jab that stiffens his legs and drives him back into the corner post. The bell sounds.

As he recovers on his stool, Tim sees that the ringcard girl from the Doll House is wearing black panties and white stilettos. The crowd cheers as she walks around.

In round number two Tim sticks George with a right hand and bloodies his lip. George replies with a big left hook that closes Tim's left eye. His peripheral vision halves. George's big bombs come from out of black space. As if that isn't enough, he feels the familiar roiling in his bowel, the urge to void himself. He clenches his muscles and bites down on his gumshield. The urge passes. He continues to stick and move around George, who holds the centre of the ring, doing nothing but waiting, waiting and watching.

Big George Foreman, who is slow and who is old, who is fat and who is fucked, whose comeback is considered a joke. Big George, who has just sold out the Eddie Graham Sports Complex, whose fight goes out on live TV. Big George, who to Tim Anderson feels like the strongest man alive.

In round number three he knocks Tim down with a big right hand that Tim doesn't see coming. The doctor checks Tim's left eye and asks him if he wants to continue. Tim says yes and bounces to the middle of the ring. George hits Tim with a body shot that almost lifts him off his feet.

In round number four, George lands a punch to the back of Tim's head that puts Tim back on the floor. Tim gets up and George punches him in the kidneys and knocks him down *again. He lands on all fours in the centre of the ring. His right eye is wide open and his left is swollen shut. His breaths are short and fast. His bowels are churning. He gets up again and raises his gloves, but the referee steps between Tim and George and waves off the fight. The crowd stand and cheer Tim's bravery. George offers a warm embrace and some consoling words.*

*'Hey, Tim,' he says, 'I didn't get that much action out of Joe Frazier.'*

*The night is a sell-out. Tim makes $3,000.*

George Foreman told the press that he wanted to fight Mike Tyson. Ron Weathers and Rick Parker talked it up. The comeback didn't seem like a joke any more. Bob Arum took a piece of Foreman alongside Ron Weathers, who had 15 per cent and Sports Day Inc., who had ten. George went to Las Vegas and knocked out Rocky Sekorski in round number three at Bally's Casino. He came back to Orlando and knocked out Tom Trimm in round number one at the Sheraton Twin Towers. He went back to Las Vegas and knocked out Guido Trane in round number five at Caesars Palace and less than six weeks later, in the same place, he knocked out Dwight Muhammad Qawi in round number seven. Then he went to Anchorage, Alaska, and knocked out Frank Lux in round number three. The comeback stood at 9 and 0 with nine knockouts. George was old and he was slow. He was fat and he was fucked. He hadn't fought anyone who stood a chance of beating him. But he had Ron Weathers and he had Bob Arum and he had Fat Rick and Sports Day Inc. To them, it lived.

*As Tim Anderson's bruises heal and his eye reopens and his adrenalin buzz dies, the fight with George Foreman seems like the start of something, an ascent, a new beginning. But when everything was over and he looked backwards he could see that it was a peak, and from it came his hurtling fall.*

Big George Foreman admires his spirit and his toughness so he hires him as a sparring partner. They work together for six weeks before George knocks out Tom Trimm in Orlando. Tim appears on the undercard, knocking out Jeff May in round number three. He registers himself at an address of Fat Rick's in Springfield, Missouri, and fights Roger Keene for the Missouri State Heavyweight title. He knocks Roger out in round number nine and wins his first championship belt. It takes six weeks to arrive, but when it comes, he takes it with him wherever he goes. His next fight is against Jimmy Young, the same Jimmy Young who beat the devil out of Big George down in San Juan in '77. Jimmy has never stopped fighting.

Perhaps he should have. Fat Rick made the fight. Tim was happy. Jimmy was a name. Then Tim hears that Fat Rick made the match because he wants Jimmy to win – so he can set up a rematch with Big George that will be a low-risk big-money fight. But Rick is supposed to be Tim's promoter, too. He is supposed to be building Tim's career, not using him to ramp George's. It comes to a head a few days before the bout. Tim arranges for himself, Jimmy Young, Jimmy's friend Floyd Patterson and another boxer called John 'The Beast' Mugabi to go to the Fort Myers High School and speak to the kids about living a clean life and staying away from drugs. Fat Rick pulls up outside the school in his limo dressed like Elvis, bombed out of his gourd on cocaine and surrounded by hookers.

Tim takes it out on Jimmy. He wins a split decision after ten rough-house rounds. It's the best victory of his career. Tired and exalted and covered in blood, Tim tells Fat Rick to screw himself. Rick laughs and says they have a signed contract. Tim takes the contract to a lawyer who tells him it's the worst he's ever seen.

Fat Rick offers him a fight with Pierre Coetzer in South Africa. He says he'll guarantee him $10,000. Tim swallows *the stuff about the contract and takes it. He travels out a month before the fight. Rick says he'll fly a trainer over later. No trainer ever shows. Coetzer is big news in Africa, he's being positioned for a world title shot, but he's never fought outside the country and he's just dropped a points decision to some guy who once lost to Evander Holyfield. His people want an American with some names on his record to restore his momentum. They offer Rick Parker $20,000. Rick takes ten for himself and promises Tim the rest. When Tim arrives in Durban, he is taken to a training camp in the middle of nowhere. He is given access to a gym that has a few heavy bags and a pair of sparring partners. He's been there about a week when he flattens one of the sparring partners and he never sees either of them again. He's left with the heavy bags and the long hours of nothing. He realises he's in trouble when the Afrikaaner guy who's been driving him round tells him that Rick has been paid off, he won't be sending a trainer. The days pass, slowly. A few hours before the fight, Fat Rick calls to wish him luck. Tim asks him about the missing trainer. Fat Rick says, 'Doc, it's not true'.*

*Tim is shadowboxing in his dressing room at West Ridge Park when two cops walk in holding rifles.*

*One says with a smile, 'Hey, man, you're gonna lose tonight, yeah?'*

*Tim laughs and says, 'I wouldn't bet on it if I was you.'*

*'Yes you are, man,' the cop says, and hits him in the face with the butt of his rifle. 'You understand?'*

*Tim feels the blood running from his nose. It drips on to his white shorts. The cops escort him through the crowd to the out-door ring. He is woozy and upset. His nose is broken. He stands in the cold while they pull the gloves on to his hands. The anthems and the intros and the bell sound distant. He can't get into the fight, can't get his mind off the cops with the guns. Pierre Coetzer catches him with some solid shots and he is counted out in round number two. He takes the microphone from the MC and tells the crowd that Coetzer punches harder than Foreman. The crowd cheer. He's taken from the dressing room by the big Afrikaaners. They drive him to a private airfield. He has nothing but the clothes he stands in. His nose is swollen and his eyes are shut.*

*They fly for ninety minutes through the African night. He's taken to a small hotel and given a room. In it are towels, mouthwash, a toothbrush and some toothpaste. Food arrives. He eats and showers and falls asleep. When he wakes up, the Afrikaaners come back and drive him to Johannesburg airport. One of them hands him his bag and his Missouri State Championship belt. The other gives him an airline ticket and his $10,000. He flies home, glad to be alive and wondering what the fuck just happened.*

*He moves from Daytona Beach to Fort Lauderdale to get away from Rick. He has very little money. Rick never actually pays him the wages he promises. Instead he always picks up the tab; Tim's never really needed any money. He still believes it will all work out. He goes back to bouncing at Summers On The Beach. He meets a girl named Gail and moves in with her. She gets pregnant so they get married before she begins to show. Soon afterwards she says she's lost the baby. Tim gives Gail all the stuff in their apartment in return for a divorce. He loses his next two fights, to Tim Morrison and Art Terry, guys who aren't fit to lace his boots. He has surgery for a deviated septum and takes time out while it heals. His divorce comes through. He gets a new girlfriend who works in a bar. It turns nasty. She dates Rick Parker out of spite. She starts a rumour that Tim is using steroids. He gives up his apartment and moves back in with his old baseball friend Jim Murphy. One day he and Jim sit down and work out how much money Fat Rick owes Tim. It adds up to $178,000.*

*'Jesus,' says Jim. 'Didn't you realise he was screwing you?'*

George Foreman knocked out Carlos Hernandez in round number four in Atlantic City. He knocked out Ladislao Mijangos in round number two in Fort Myers and then Bobby Hitz in round number one in Auburn Hills. He knocked out Tony Fulilangi in round number two in Marshall, Texas and then David Jaco in round number one in Bakersfield, California. He knocked out Mark Young in round number seven in Rochester, New York, then Manoel de Almeida in round number three in Orlando and then JB Williamson in round number five in Galveston, Texas.

George took his first fight against a meaningful opponent. His name was Smokin' Bert Cooper. Bert punched so hard, he'd been signed by Joe Frazier, who thought he could train Bert up as a champion. Joe sold his collection of motorcycles to buy Bert a car. Bert slowly disabused Joe of his vision. Joe gave up and cut his losses.

Now Bert was an opponent for George. They were to fight in Phoenix, Arizona. Bert was relaxing in his hotel room a couple of days beforehand when he answered a knock on the door. Standing there were three hot girls loaded with booze and blow. Bert thought he'd died and gone to heaven. They partied right up until the fight. He didn't sleep for seventy-two hours. Didn't need to. When the bout started, he had nothing left at all. George clipped him a couple of times, and he stayed on his stool, unable to answer the bell for round number two. His urine test came back positive for marijuana and cocaine. The Arizona State Athletic Commission withheld his purse until he'd spent eight weeks in rehab. Big George Foreman's comeback stood at 18 and 0 with 18 stoppages. He weighed 252 pounds. He was old and he was slow. He was fat and he was fucked. But no one was laughing any more.

*Bob Arum cuts Fat Rick out of the George Foreman comeback, the comeback that Rick Parker believed in and Bob Arum did* *not. Fat Rick decides to fuck Bob Arum right back. Big George's next fight is against Gerry Cooney in Atlantic City. George knocks Gerry out in round number two. As he leaves the ring, Jack Solloway, this big, clever kid Rick's been using as a bodyguard, jumps out of the crowd, sticks a lawsuit to George Foreman's chest and says, 'You're served'. Fat Rick withholds George's purse. He sues Ron Weathers, Bob Arum, Top Rank Inc., Caesars World Inc., Caesars Sports Inc., Caesars New Jersey Inc. and anyone else he can think of. Bob Arum threatens all kind of hell. Rick keeps his nerve. Bob Arum settles the lawsuit with a cheque for $150,000.*

*Fuck you very much, Bob.*

*Fuck you very much, George.*

*Under the terms of settlement Sports Day Inc. has to surrender all past, current and future claims on the career of George Foreman. Fat Rick doesn't give a fuck about that. He signs the papers and takes his cheque to the bank. Doug and Joyce Davis are left with a 10 per cent share of nothing. They lose their $50,000. They lose their bar.*

*Fuck you very much, Doug.*

*Fuck you very much, Joyce.*

*This is boxing. It isn't like normal life. It doesn't work that way.*

*He meets Rob Russen in Fort Myers at one of Tim Anderson's fights. Rob is managing a stable of heavyweights that includes Smokin' Bert Cooper, David 'Hand Grenade' Bey and Oliver 'The Atomic Bull' McCall. Rick sees the chance to get straight back into the game. He offers Rob Russen the vice-presidency of Rick Parker Presents . . . his newly formed promotional company. Rob Russen accepts. They set up training camp in Tampa in the sun. A brand new start.*

*The Rick Parker dream, still intact. The Rick Parker vision, shimmering and alive.*

*He gets loaded on cocaine because it takes him past the*

*barriers, way out beyond the boundaries of his fear and his doubt, it takes him to the place where he can say fuck you Bob Arum, fuck you George Foreman, where he can cut free from the solitude of his strangeness. This is why he loves it so.*

*He buys himself flashy new clothes. Bomber jackets and boxy suits. High-collared shirts and Cuban heel boots, white flared trousers and skin-tight vests. The Elvis shades with their jewelled frames. The final pieces of his puzzle. An image they'll never forget. The man he always wanted to be.*

*He visits a jeweller and commissions a new piece, a great gold boxing glove on a solid gold chain. He wears it tight around his neck, his totem, his statement, his vision. There is money in his pocket, there is a fervour in his mind. The dream is his and his alone.*

*Tim Anderson turns his great strength inwards.*

*One night he says to Jim Murphy, 'I'll get it.'*

*'Get what?'*

*'The $178,000.'*

*'Oh yeah?' says Jim.*

*'Oh yeah,' says Tim.*

*He makes his vow. He holds it to his heart. He will find his own way now. He will make good his losses. He will find resolve in defeat and adversity, just as he always has. He will get his money and build a house, a house for Erin in the Florida sun.*

# Rick Parker Presents . . .

Rob Russen went to New York to find Mitch 'Blood' Green. Fat Rick asked him to do it. Mitch was in Harlem at the time. Rick heard that Mitch was in possession of a letter that promised him a fight with Mike Tyson for the world heavyweight championship, signed by Tyson's management. Mitch had already fought Mike twice. The first time was a loss on points just before Mike became champ. The second was after Mike had stretched Michael Spinks. It happened outside a clothes shop called Dapper Dan's in Harlem at 4 a.m. Mike broke his knuckles on Mitch's head. That was how Mitch was supposed to have got the letter, as a part of a deal not to file assault charges against Mike. Rick wanted the letter and he wanted Mitch Green.

Rob flew to New York and drove to Harlem and found Mitch. He wasn't hard to spot. He was six feet five and 250 pounds with long jerry curls and more jewellery than Fat Rick. Rob got him on a plane back to Tampa. Fat Rick went to work on Mitch Green. He got hold of the letter promising Mitch a fight with Mike. He gave Mitch a $5,000 signing bonus and a wage of five hundred a week. He provided a furnished apartment and a car. All Mitch had to do was get back in shape, knock a couple of guys over and let Fat Rick handle the rest.

They had a launch for the press at a gym in Tampa. Mitch wore a T-shirt that said 'Mike Tyson Is A Homo' on the front. He gave the press chapter and verse on Iron Mike and Don King. He worked out impressively on the heavy bag. Rick predicted he'd have the fight with Mike on within a year. The papers bit. The next day's headlines were full of Mitch Green and Fat Rick and the stable of heavyweights coming to Tampa under the brand new banner, Rick Parker Presents . . .

Don Hazelton became Executive Director of the Florida State Athletic Commission in 1988 by a vote of four commissioners to one. He had the perfect résumé for the job. He was a former member of the Florida House of Representatives and an ex-private detective. He had eighteen fights as an amateur boxer on his record. He was determined to make Florida a safe place to box. He aimed to make it incorruptible. He attended almost every card in the state himself. He introduced stringent measures to clean it up. He started two hundred enforcement actions a year against boxers, promoters, trainers and managers. He operated a zero tolerance policy on everything, from attending weigh-ins late to failing random drug tests. His first confrontation with Fat Rick came when he refused thirty-nine-year-old Jimmy Young a licence to box on a Rick Parker card at JJ Whispers in Orlando. Jimmy was so out of shape he could hardly get his shorts up over his stomach. Fat Rick threatened legal action. He told Don Hazelton, 'You can do that in Russia, but you can't do it here'. Don Hazelton did it anyway. Jimmy Young never fought again. Don Hazelton began to watch Rick Parker closely.

Mitch Green was costing Fat Rick money, shacked up in his furnished apartment, driving his brand new car, telling everyone that Mike Tyson was a pussy and a homo without doing any actual fighting. Three or four times he'd pulled out of comeback bouts at the last minute. Not even Rob Russen could tie him down. Rob, who always had his eye on the ball, who didn't drink, didn't smoke, didn't do drugs. A detail man. Rick Parker's perfect foil.

Fat Rick got frustrated and fucked off. He set up a show at Finkies nightclub in Daytona Beach. He made it as simple as he could for Mitch. He gave him an exhibition fight against a local car dealer buried in the middle of the bill.

Fat Rick saw an easy night ahead for everyone. He got blitzed and cruised down to Finkies for the fights, right into a shitstorm he hadn't seen coming. Don fucking Hazelton of the Florida State Athletic Commission was already there, stomping around and squeaking and squawking because the crowd were in the building and no one had set the ring up. There were no gloves, stools or anything else. Don said he'd cancel the show and refund the gate money if the ring was not up in an hour. Fat Rick smiled and told Don it was all under control. He found Rob Russen. He made some calls. The ring went up with minutes to spare. No panic, baby. Bert Cooper knocked out Rick Hoard in round number one. Buster Drayton outpointed Daryl Fromm. Mitch Green had a fight too, but it wasn't with the car dealer. Mitch was parading around telling everyone what he was going to do to Mike Tyson when Kevin Rooney, Mike Tyson's trainer, showed up.

Mitch began to taunt him. 'Do you kiss Mike on the lips? Are you a faggot boy too?' Kevin Rooney went for Mitch Green. He chased him through the crowd. Mitch Green started pushing and shoving Kevin. Other boxers jumped between them. The crowd cheered. Fat Rick watched the chaos, felt the money falling out of his pocket and vowed to cut Mitch Green loose as soon as he could make his investment back.

Smokin' Bert Cooper was nothing like Mitch. He was a street guy, too, but he would fight anyone, anywhere, anytime, just as long as he made a cheque. He'd blown it with Joe Frazier, the cars and the money had gone, and now he was living in a mobile home in Roanoke, Virginia. Boxing was all that he knew. Bert was a fuck-up, but he was a fuck-up who could punch. He had a magic right hand, a blurring wand that sent big guys to sleep. Fat Rick understood the street and he understood Bert Cooper. He sent him $50 per day via Western Union because $50 per day was enough for Bert to eat and buy a six pack but not enough for him to buy hard drugs or alcohol.

*Rick Parker takes control of the life and career of Smokin' Bert Cooper. He knows what he needs: money in his pocket, dreams in his head, Rick Parker in his heart. With Rob Russen, he begins to rebuild Bert's career. They get him a fight for the NABF heavyweight title against Orlin Norris. Bert knocks out Orlin in round number eight but loses the belt in his next fight, a narrow decision to Ray Mercer. Fat Rick does not take a cut from Bert's purses. He jokes around and calls Bert '$50 Bert' behind his back but he believes; he believes in Bert Cooper and his magic right hand.*

*He and Rob get Bert $75,000 to fight Riddick Bowe, who is an Olympic silver medallist and unbeaten in nineteen fights. They fly to Las Vegas. Bert brings his girlfriend Dolphine. She and Bert fight all the way up to the fight. In round number one Bert rips into Riddick Bowe but Riddick survives. Rob Russen watches Bert scan the crowd for Dolphine as he sits on his stool, love in his eyes. In round number two, Bert glances down for Dolphine again and Riddick lands a tremendous right hand that knocks Bert out. By the time Bert and*

*Dolphine leave Las Vegas, the $75,000 is gone. They borrow the money to get back to Roanoke, and wait for Fat Rick's next $50 to arrive.*

*This is boxing, thinks Rick. This is not normal life.*

*Big George Foreman gets his title shot on 19 April 1991 when he fights Evander Holyfield in Atlantic City. George loses a unanimous decision. 1.4 million people buy the pay per view. The windfall factor, millions and millions, all in one night. Fat Rick watches the fight on TV. He burns with vindication. He burns with the injustice of it. He gets high and he gets mad. He is not finished with George Foreman. He has a greater purpose. He has a grander vision.*

*Rick Parker does not forget what Don King told him. He finds a new fighter, a white fighter, a white heavyweight, a white giant, a white champion. The fighter's name is Mark Gastineau. He is a seven-time All Pro defensive end with the New York Jets. He holds the all-time single season sack record in the NFL. Mark is six feet five inches tall and 250 pounds. He is handsome and he is famous. He is rich and he is marketable. The few people in America who don't know Mark for playing football know him because he stole Sylvester Stallone's ex-wife Brigitte Neilsen and went on all the TV talk shows to boast about it. He and Brigitte had a son together called Killian and matching tattoos on their buttocks. Then Mark broke up with Brigitte. He wants to show her what she is missing but he doesn't know how. He decides to try boxing and gets himself a trainer called Jimmy Glenn.*

*Fat Rick wages a four-month campaign of flattery and persuasion on Mark, Mark's father Ernie and Jimmy Glenn. He offers Mark $5,000 a month plus a minimum of $5,000 per fight to sign a contract with Rick Parker Presents . . . He offers Jimmy Glenn five hundred per week and his assistant Willie Dunn three hundred per week. He calls Ron Weathers.*

*He tells Ron that a fight between Mark Gastineau and George*
*Foreman will make both boxers a minimum of $5 million. Ron*
*Weathers laughs and tells Fat Rick that if he can get*
*Gastineau to 12 and 0 they'll talk about a fight. Fat Rick takes*
*that as a guarantee.*

*Rob Russen calls his old friend Derrick 'Starfire' Dukes and*
*offers him $600 to be Mark Gastineau's first professional*
*opponent. Derrick is a pro wrestler and knows exactly how to*
*work the press. 'I've beaten up bigger guys than Mark*
*Gastineau on the street,' he tells them.*
  *They fight at the Civic Centre in Salem, Virginia. Fat Rick*
*goes to Derrick Dukes' dressing room before the fight and tells*
*him, 'as soon as a strong wind blows, get the hell out of there'.*
*Derrick Dukes is flattened by the second punch of Mark*
*Gastineau's new career. He goes down just the way he was*
*taught in wrestling school, his chin tucked in, his legs flying*
*up, his back making a loud slap on the canvas.*
  *Fat Rick tells the press that Derrick Dukes has been taken to*
*hospital. A reporter named Jay Marioti says he wasn't because*
*he just met Derrick Dukes at the airport terminal. Four days*
*later the Virginia commissioner Mike Beaver clears the fight*
*after viewing a tape. Mark Gastineau is 1 and 0. George*
*Foreman is eleven fights away.*

*Fat Rick gets himself a new bodyguard. His name is Sonny*
*Barch. Sonny has fast hands and a loose temper. Rick finds*
*him selling cars at Gossett Motors in Memphis, Tennessee.*
*Sonny's boxing career has stalled at 19 and 3, but he's big*
*and he's white so Rick tells him he'll start him back. Rick sets*
*him up in training and gives him plenty of odd jobs to do.*
*Sonny collects money, Sonny makes calls, Sonny talks up fight*
*cards to the local press men. Most of all, Sonny hangs out with*
*Fat Rick partying. Sonny is Rick's can-do man. And Sonny is*
*a crossroader.*

*Fat Rick finds Bert Cooper a fight with Joe Hipp in Atlantic City. Joe Hipp is supposed to be going places in the heavyweight division, but after Bert has finished with him, Joe looks like he's been in a car accident. $50 Bert is back. Fat Rick disappears into the black heart of Atlantic City with his tiny gun in his silver case and scores some celebratory blow. He gets high, high, high, he is lost in his reverie, a reverie that lasts for months and months as his visions are made real . . .*

*Let them fear him now. Let them know him now. Don King and Bob Arum. Dan Duva and Don Hazelton. Rob Russen and all his fussing about office hours and business strategy. His crows and his ravens and his rooks . . .*

*Evander Holyfield signs to fight Mike Tyson in what will be Evander's first defence since beating George Foreman, but Mike gets his ribs broken by a sparring partner named Garing Lane. Fat Rick phones Dan Duva, Evander's manager, five times a day and sends a long fax once a day listing the reasons why Bert Cooper should replace Mike Tyson. Fat Rick calls and he faxes and he begs and he pleads, but Dan and Evander choose an Italian guy, Francesco Damiani, instead, an Italian guy who Rick's never heard of.*

*Then the Italian guy sprains an ankle and flies home and Dan Duva is back on the phone asking for Bert, offering the fight, paying him $350,000 even though the Italian guy was getting $750,000 and Rick says yes anyway because he knows that this is it, here it is, this is the chance to show them: Dan Duva and Don King, Don Hazelton and Bob Arum, the doubters and the gloaters, the haters and the jokers who laughed at him and stole his fighters and said no, not you, not here, not in this business, not in our business, not this way.*

*Bert hasn't trained for a month and when he gets flu two days before the fight, he doesn't tell anyone but Rick who takes him to a clinic and pays the doctor to give Bert some flu medicine and keep his mouth shut.*

*Ten p.m. on 23 November 1991 at the Omni, Atlanta. $50 Bert
is up against the ropes in round number three and taking
Evander Holyfield's best shots when he sees a gap between the
punches and throws a right hook, a right hook from that magic
right hand. It lands high on the side of Evander's head. The
champion of the world grabs on to the top rope with his right
glove to stop himself from going down for the first time in his
career. Referee Mills Lane gives Evander a standing eight count
even though this is a fight for the WBA Championship and
WBA fights do not have standing eight counts in their rules.
The standing eight count seems to go on forever. Rick Parker
slaps the ring apron with his fat white hand and screams at
Bert to fuck the eight count, fuck the eight count and finish
him, finish him, finish him here, finish him now, because this
is it, this is it, baby . . . right here and right now.*

*$50 Bert sucks up some air and throws as many punches as
he can at Evander Holyfield's head, but Evander's got his
senses back and he holds on and holds on and smothers and
smothers until the bell rings and the round ends and his mind
clears.*

*In round number five Bert gets on top again, driving Evander
into the ropes with some hard punches, but Mills Lane stops the
action when he sees a tear in Evander's right glove. Bert stands
in a neutral corner while the glove is changed. The delay lasts
for three minutes because Lou Duva, who is Evander's
cornerman and Dan Duva's brother, begins taking off the left
glove instead of the right. When the fight starts again Bert
blows himself out, blows himself out because he has the flu and
he hasn't trained for a month and he lives in a mobile home in
Roanoke, Virginia, on $50 a day. Mills Lane stops the contest
in round number seven after Bert takes twenty-three consecutive
shots to the head.*

*Don King tries to lure Bert Cooper away – which would shut
Rick Parker out. Shut him out and shut him up. Shut him up*

*and shut him down. Don flies Bert's co-manager Jimmy Adams and his attorney Doug Henson to New York. He gives them the Don King treatment. He tells the press that Bert Cooper is the uncrowned heavyweight champion of the world. He tells them that Dan Duva and Mills Lane stole the world title away from him, stole it away with their standing eight count, the standing eight count that shouldn't have happened in a WBA-sanctioned bout. He advances Bert some money and signs him up to a two-fight deal. Don King calls Rick Parker and invites him to a meeting at the Marriott Hotel in Boca Raton. It's the week before Christmas 1991. Don arrives with his stepson, Carl. Rick Parker is already there, grey suit and a bright white shirt, paisley tie and cowboy boots, sunglasses on and hair teased up, ready to meet his hero, ready to meet Don King.*

*Don tells Rick that Bert would rather retire than fight for Rick Parker again. Instead, Bert wants to take a tune-up fight in Las Vegas in February and then he wants to fight Donovan 'Razor' Ruddock on pay-per-view TV for a million dollars. Rick knows that Razor Ruddock is the last person on earth that Bert Cooper should fight. He's too short and he's too strong. And anyhow Rick's already signed an agreement with Dan Duva for Bert to fight Michael Moorer instead.*

*Don King and Razor Ruddock. Dan Duva and Michael Moorer. The doubters and the haters. The haters and the gloaters. The crows in the freeway margins.*

*Don King talks for four hours. He says he'll pay Rick money to step aside as Bert's sole promoter. He'll allow Rick to work with Don King Productions. He'll give Fat Rick Parker the keys to the kingdom of heaven if Rick will do this one small thing for him. Rick Parker rolls the dice. He gets paid by Don King. He screws Dan Duva. He signs a two-fight deal for Bert to fight Cecil Coffee at the Mirage Hotel in Las Vegas in February and then an unspecified opponent to be approved by him on a date to be announced. He reneges on the agreement with Dan Duva for Bert to fight Michael Moorer. But he still gets paid. Carl King takes stacks of new bills from a blue canvas bag and hands them to Rick, still in their Federal Reserve wrappings. Carl gives him two post-dated cheques for the balance due.*

*Don King and Razor Ruddock. Dan Duva and Michael Moorer.*

*Don King's first cheque bounces.*

*Dan Duva sues Rick Parker for $3.5 million.*

*When Rick gets to Las Vegas for Bert Cooper versus Cecil Coffee, Don King is not there. Rick has not been booked into the Mirage Hotel with the rest of the entourage. Rick has not been given any meal tickets. Rick has not been given any fight tickets. He gets ahold of Don King and they meet for breakfast on the day of the fight. Don tells Rick that the second bout of Bert Cooper's two-fight deal must be against Razor Ruddock or he can't make any money from the contract.*

*Rick Parker says, 'No way, Don, no way. I told you before . . .'*

*Don King says: 'I like you, Rick Parker. That's a million-dollar gamble. By the way, I've stopped payment on your second cheque.'*

*Bert Cooper breaks Cecil Coffee's nose and knocks him out in round number two. Rick Parker meets Dan Duva at the Hilton Hotel in Wilmington, Delaware, and remakes the agreement for Bert Cooper to fight Michael Moorer for the WBO Heavyweight Championship of the World in Atlantic City.*

*Rick Parker gets paid by Dan Duva. Fat Rick screws Don King.*

*$50 Bert is staying at the Days Inn Suites in Philadelphia two months before the fight with Michael Moorer when ten big men turn up and tell him he needs to speak to Don King right now. Bert gets spooked. He moves his training camp three times across three states. He receives a lawsuit from Don King Productions. By the time he arrives at the Trump Taj Mahal in*

*Atlantic City for the fight, three members of his entourage are wearing bullet-proof vests.*

*Don King receives a lawsuit from Bert Cooper. Don King gets spooked. The weekend before the fight between $50 Bert and Michael Moorer, he calls police to his house on E62 Street in New York. He tells them that there are hit men outside his door, hit men sent to kill him. The men turn out to be process servers. Don King fucking freaks out. He says, 'It's all part of an insidious plot to destroy Don King. They got the perfect guy to try to bring me down. We all know what Bert Cooper is into. It must have really messed him up.'*

*Don King and Donovan Ruddock. Dan Duva and Michael Moorer. Rick Parker and Bert Cooper. Ready for battle, ready for war.*

*The fight with Michael Moorer takes place amid an atmosphere of paranoia and fear. Bert knocks Michael down in round number one, but Michael gets up and knocks Bert down, too. They go back and forth with hard, hard punches. By the end of round number five, Bert is done. Michael hits him with five unanswered blows to the head and the fight is stopped.*

*Rick and Bert. Bert and Rick. Never again so close. Never again so near. Rick does not realise it yet. He thinks there will be more. He feels there will be more, he fucking knows there will be more, because he is Fat Rick, he is Rick Parker, he is Elvis. Many more nights like these, with Bert, with Mark Gastineau, with Rick Parker Presents . . .*

*He goes back to his hotel room on a shimmering, snowblind high. He plugs in his keyboard and he plays and he sings, he sings and he plays, his big, fat hands pressing down on the keys, his high Southern voice soaring over the top. He plays the songs that he knows, the songs that he loves, as loud as he likes. Fat Rick plays Bob Seger. Fat Rick plays Neil Diamond. Fat Rick plays Elvis, baby. Fat Rick plays Elvis.*

# Part Two

# The Years of
# the Locust

Tim Anderson with Suzanne Migdall, shortly before his fight wth Larry Holmes (*courtesy Suzanne Migdall*)

# Kayfabe

## i. San Francisco

Fat Rick, sleeping late, woken at last by his rasping snores. Beached on the king-size, afloat in his night sweats, he comes round slowly, slowly, slowly. He walks to the window of his hotel room. He opens the drapes and lets in the sun. Always sunny in San Francisco. This city of peace, this city of love. Its bright, hot skies. He showers and dresses and straightens up his hair. Bright white sneakers and bright white slacks. Bright white vest and a blue bomber jacket. The Elvis hair. Those Elvis shades.

The air con hums. The clock ticks. He calls down for coffee and he sits and he drinks. The great gold boxing glove around his neck. The Glock 9mm in its silver case.

Rick Parker, dressed for battle. Rick Parker, ready for war.

Mark Gastineau is 9 and 0. Big George Foreman, three fights away. Three fights away. Mark's next fight is at the San Francisco Civic Auditorium in five nights' time. It's live on coast-to-coast TV on ABC Television's *Tuesday Night Fights*. His national debut. His big step up. The night he becomes a championship contender. The night America sees what Rick Parker sees.

Three more fights. Three more wins. Always on his mind.

Three more fights, three more wins. This revenge. This war.

What the world sees and what the world does not. Mark Gastineau is the fulfilment of what Don King told Rick Parker. He is six feet five and weighs 256. He's two inches taller than George Foreman. He's ten pounds heavier than George Foreman. He has 4 per cent body fat. He can run forty yards in 4.6 seconds. He can pick up a sixteen-stone quarterback and pound him into the ground so hard that the quarterback thinks he might never breathe again. He is an athlete. He is a star. In consecutive fights from 8 June 1991 to 3 March 1992 he knocks out Derrick Dukes in round number one, Mike Acklie in round number two, Tim Murphy in round number two, Chuck Nail in round number one, Jimmy Baker in round number two and then Jimmy Baker again in round number one, Kevin Barch in round number one, Troy Berg in round number one and Lon Liebergen in round number one.

Mark knocks out his first nine opponents in twelve rounds. Mike Tyson knocks out his first nine opponents in sixteen rounds. George Foreman wins his first nine fights in thirty-seven rounds. Muhammad Ali wins his first nine fights in forty-nine rounds. Mark Gastineau is big and famous and white and 9 and 0, three fights away.

What the world sees and what the world does not. Mark is full of rage and doubt. Mark has congenital psoriasis. Mark gets jacked up on steroids. Fat Rick pays Derrick Dukes $600 to take a dive in Mark's first bout. He pays Tim Murphy $1,500 to take a dive in his third. He pays Kevin Barch $1,000 to do the same in his seventh. Derrick Dukes, Chuck Nail, Tim Murphy, Kevin Barch and Troy Berg have never had a professional fight before they fight Mark. Jimmy Baker has had one professional fight before he fights Mark twice. Of Mark Gastineau's first nine opponents, only three, including Jimmy two-times, have ever entered a ring before. Of Mark Gastineau's first nine opponents, only two have ever won a fight. By the time Mark gets to 9 and 0, he has won more fights than all of his opponents put together.

Fat Rick has the *Tuesday Night Fights* people in his ear, calling on his cell phone, calling to tell him that there are five days to go and Mark Gastineau still has no opponent. Rick knows that. He tells them not to worry. He tells them he has options. He tells them it's under control

Fat Rick gets them off the fucking phone. He sits and he thinks. The clock ticks. The sun streams into his hotel room.

'Who should he fight,' he thinks 'Who can Mark fight in five nights' time?'

The single most important decision in the boxing career of Mark Gastineau . . .

The single most important decision in the promotional career of Rick Parker . . . for Fat Rick's dreams of a white heavyweight champion . . . for Fat Rick's dream of the windfall factor . . .

Who should he fight . . . who should he fight . . .

The clock ticks and the sun streams in. The phone rings and he ignores it.

Who can he control? Who can he trust? Who needs money? Who has names on his record, names that will look good on Mark Gastineau's record, names that the television commentators can read out to their nationwide audience?

The sun dies. The clock ticks. Fat Rick gets high and calls Tim Anderson.

Things have levelled out for Tim. He has a new manager, Suzanne Migdall, who owns Summers On The Beach. Suzanne has never been a boxing manager before but she arranges a fight with Larry Holmes, who's making a come-back. Larry breaks two of Tim's ribs in round number one, but he admires Tim's guts and Tim leaves the ring with honour. It's a happy day, a good day. While his ribs heal up, he's offered some work on a film, playing a boxer.

It's 2 a.m. EST when the call comes in. Jim Murphy rouses Tim from his spare room. Rick Parker roars down the line.

'Uh, Rick,' he says in his sleep-filled voice, 'I can't do it. I'm making a movie at the moment. I'm contracted to these people. I'm not in shape. I haven't trained. I . . .'

Ah, Timmy. He never could see the bigger picture. The Rick Parker picture . . .

'A movie? What fucking movie? You an actor or a fighter? I can't believe we're having this conversation. You losin' it, buddy? This is LIVE TV, BABY – NATIONWIDE . . . Was your fight with Foreman on national TV? Was your fight with Holmes on national TV? No, sir. What you waiting for, man?'

Rick hits the notes he needs to hit. He offers to pay Tim Anderson the $178,000 he owes him. He offers to fly in his trainer Bill Lucci from Canada. He offers to put them up in a good hotel. He offers to smooth it over with the producers of the movie. He offers to put Doc Anderson on *Tuesday Night Fights*, live across America.

Rick gets on the phone to the movie producers and sells them the dream. The boxer in their film, fighting live on coast-to-coast TV. Publicity it's hard to buy. The movie guys film Tim's outstanding scenes in two days. Tim flies to San Francisco. He checks into his nice hotel. Bill Lucci shows up. Bill says that Mark Gastineau has never gone past two rounds in his life. If Tim can take him into the third, fourth, fifth, they've got him.

Rick fills his silver case with as much money as he can fit inside and takes it to Tim Anderson's hotel room. He lays it on the table, unopened.

Rick tells Tim how it's going to go down on *Tuesday Night Fights*: Mark Gastineau knocks out Doc Anderson. Doc tells the *Tuesday Night Fights* fans that Mark Gastineau hit him harder than Larry Holmes and Big George Foreman did.

Mark Gastineau will be 10 and 0, big and famous, handsome and white. George Foreman, big and black and on the road to winning his title back. The greatest story in boxing. Mark versus George, white versus black, millions of dollars, all at one time.

Tim Anderson's kickback: $500,000, in cash, paid to him on the day that Mark fights George.

Tim says nothing. Rick comes up with more. Tim and Mark will make a boxing fitness video together. Rick will prevail upon Tex Cobb to get Tim more movie roles. Tim still says nothing so Rick takes out the cell phone and makes a call. The guy on the other end is a business adviser for George Foreman. Rick hands the phone to Tim. George's man says, 'You know something, kid? You're never going to make money like this again in your life. Half a million dollars takes care of you, your sister, your family, everything. Think about it.'

Tim hands the phone back to Rick. Rick says, 'Don't worry, it's a done deal', and hangs up. He opens the silver case. Inside are stacks of hundred-dollar bills, still wrapped. He shows them to Tim. He tells Tim that everything is going to be okay, all okay in San Francisco, this city of peace, this city of love.

Fat Rick back in his hotel room, the air con humming, the day dying, the business done. He lays out his keyboard on the king-size bed and sets about it, singing Neil Diamond numbers as the night comes down.

Tim goes for a run. He hits the heavy bag and he makes the speedball thrum. Rick Parker's offer is on his mind, the Elvis voice is back in his ear, the Foreman connection is making him think.

*– He accepts the offer and lays down in front of Mark Gastineau. Rick gives him the money he saw in the case. Mark fights George and he gets the rest. He lives with the knowledge that he threw a fight. Erin lives in a brand new house . . .*

*– He takes a bath on national TV, Mark fights George, George destroys Mark and Rick pays Tim nothing. Tim is tainted goods . . .*

*– He lays down in front of Mark, Mark loses his next fight and there is no fight with George. Tim is marked by the fix . . .*

*– He fights Mark and he wins, Fat Rick pays him nothing and destroys his career . . .*

Tim finds a payphone and tells Jim Murphy that Rick Parker just offered him half a million dollars to take a dive on live TV.

Jim laughs and asks Tim if he's got it in writing.

Rick comes to Tim's hotel room at 11 a.m. on the day of the fight. Rick Parker, with Mark Gastineau standing behind him. Rick says, 'Mark wants to talk about the fight.'

Tim says, 'Well, we're fighting.' He looks at Mark. 'I'm gonna knock your ass out.'

Rick smiles. Rick laughs. 'You crazy, Doc? Perhaps you are.'

Marty Sammon takes a call from the Athletic Commission telling him that he'll be refereeing Mark Gastineau versus Tim Anderson. Marty has been a referee for fifteen years. He's refereed a thousand fights plus. He's been hearing that Mark Gastineau's fights are not on the level.

Marty goes to Tim's hotel room too. He says, 'Look me in the eye and tell me nothing's going on.'

Tim says, 'Oh, they tried, but I'll tell you what I told them.

I'm a man of honour, and I'm fighting. I don't lay down for anyone. I'm going to win this fight.'

Marty says, 'Okay, Tim, I'll hold you to that.'

What the cameras see and what the cameras do not. Tim Anderson stands in a small, bright room at the San Francisco Civic Auditorium just before 6 p.m. He looks at his body in the long wall mirror. This fighter's body, pale and hard. Made by the speedball and the heavy bag. Made on the road. Made in the gym. Made in the ring. Made with love and hurt. Made to honour his father and his mother. Made to protect his sister. Made for nights like this one.

He has the gloves pulled over his bandaged hands. He has the gloves laced and knotted. He has the knots covered with tape. He taps his gloves together.

He shadowboxes two rounds. He's warm and covered by a fine sweat.

Marty Sammon comes into the dressing room. 'I'm telling you what I just told him,' Marty says, 'there better be no monkey business tonight. No one will lay down in my ring and still get paid.'

'No, sir,' he says quietly. 'No, sir, never. Not me. I'm here to fight'.

And he is, he is.

Fat Rick comes into Tim's dressing room. Charcoal suit and a mustard shirt. Open neck and shiny shoes. The great red hairpiece on his head. The silver case in his fat right hand.

Tim thinks, okay, here it is, here he comes.

But all Rick says is, 'Hey, Tim, what you wearing? I'll give you five hundred for your robe and trunks, because Mark's forgotten his . . .'

Mark Gastineau in his own small, bright room at the Civic Auditorium, Jimmy Ellis holding the pads, Willie Dunn with a towel on his shoulders, Mark stripped to the waist and wearing cut-down sweatpants because he's forgotten to bring his fucking shorts. His hands are floating in the foreign gloves, his feet are sweating in the foreign boots. The TV camera is in his face, the fight fans waiting to see what he's got, Tim Anderson two doors down, ready to fight, ready to go in this city of peace, in this city of love.

In homes across America, the *Tuesday Night Fights* telecast begins. The *Tuesday Night Fights* fans see a montage of Mark Gastineau playing football for the Jets. They see Mark and Brigitte walking in the park. Brigitte wears a leather skirt. Mark wears leather trousers.

The announcer says, 'And now, at the age of thirty-six, with Brigitte and the football career behind him, Gastineau has found a new love . . . in the ring, far beyond the football wars.'

A TV guy gives Tim the word. Out of the dressing room and down the corridor, along the dark walkways between the seats, towards the ring, towards the light. He is wearing his blue and yellow satin robe and his blue and yellow satin shorts. He has his hair drawn back in a small ponytail. He sees Rick Parker by the ring apron. He walks on by, towards the steps and towards the rope. As he passes Fat Rick he says, 'Your guy better be able to fight . . .'

The *Tuesday Night Fights* viewers watch Mark's pre-recorded interview. 'It's like apples and oranges,' he says about football and boxing. 'Stepping in Shea or the Meadowlands, I was stepping in with people who weren't a hundred per cent for me. When I step in the ring Jimmy's behind me with his hands on my shoulders, Willie's beside me, I got people that are there for me one hundred per cent and they want to see me do good. It's like day and night. I love stepping into the ring compared to stepping out on the field.'

They ask Mark, 'Some say your boxing career is just a carnival sideshow.'

Mark says, 'If being in a carnival is as hard work as what I'm putting in, I tell you what, I have a lot of respect for carnival people. As far as the exposure, if I'm never talked about in the papers or never seen on TV again, that would not bother me one bit, and that comes from my heart.'

Sean O'Grady and Al Albert call the fight from ringside. Mark steps through the ropes and into the ring wearing a short black robe and the cut-down pants. Rick Parker climbs up on to the ring apron and leans over the top rope. The camera dwells on him as Al Albert says, 'Mark considers he's ready for prime time, but consider Sean, he's ready for prime time on his terms. Carefully selected opponents and the carefully selected opponent tonight is the veteran Tim "Doc" Anderson.'

Tim's picture appears on the screen next to Mark's. His record displayed beneath: 25-15-1, 13 KOs.

'Twenty-five wins,' says Al Albert, 'but most of those came early in his career against cruiserweights. Lately he's been a sacrificial lamb on the comeback plate of the likes of George Foreman, who stopped him in four, and Larry Holmes, who stopped him in one, but of course those two with ex-world champion experience, and Anderson feels he has the know-how against his big-name but novice opponent.'

The bell sounds. Tim skips from his corner to the centre of the ring, loose and alive. Mark thuds from his with his mouth open, his muscles tight, his hands in the foreign gloves, his feet in the foreign boots. After two minutes and thirty-four seconds of round number one, Sean O'Grady says, 'Mark actually forgot his trunks for this bout. If you look closely you can see he's wearing cut-downs.'

Al Albert says, 'I don't know if you can hear it at home, but the crowd is starting to boo Mark Gastineau.'

Mark throws an uppercut that misses Tim by three feet. Tim tries not to laugh.

In the corner on his stool between the rounds, mouth open, eyes closed, Mark hears Jimmy Glenn saying: 'Just throw your hands. What I need is you to try to knock this guy's head off. Move your hands. You gotta walk in and throw punches, alright?'

Mark has stayed up all night arguing with his girlfriend Missy. He's thinking, 'I've gotta get a new girlfriend.'

In round number two, Mark, the lost boy miles from home, mouth open and muscles tense, the words of Jimmy Glenn in his ears, the argument with Missy on his mind, can't hit Tim, can't reach him, can't knock his head off like he did Derrick Dukes the wrestler and Kevin Barch the crane driver and Troy Berg who'd never had a fight. Tim throws a looping right hand that hits Mark's glove before it hits his head but the weight of the punch is enough to spin him onto the ropes. Mark drops his hands and turns his back to Tim. Tim hits him hard in the mouth with a left hand swung around the corner.

Sean O'Grady says, 'Here's an example of a fighter not knowing what to do when he gets hit.'

Mark begins round number three with a straight left, his best punch of the fight. Tim blitzes him back with a hard right and a harder left. Mark gets Tim in a headlock. Mark's mouth is open. His eyes are wide. He has never been past round number two in his life. Tim hits Mark with a left hand and Mark collapses on the ring post in his corner. Marty Sammon gives him a count. As he does, Marty thinks to himself, 'Geez, I don't think Mark Gastineau could knock me out.'

With nine seconds left in round number four Tim drives Mark to the ropes once more. Mark looks at Marty Sammon because he wants Marty to save his ass, but Marty is not there to do that job. Tim watches Mark's eyes leave his own and lets go with a long left. Mark drops to the floor, his eyes closed, his mouth open, his gumshield out, his brains scrambled on coast-to-coast TV.

Fat Rick watches Marty Sammon help Mark to his feet. He does not hear the bell sound, he does not hear Marty's count finish at number eight. He is thinking, five thousand per month for Mark who has been beaten, five hundred per week for Jimmy Glenn and three hundred per week for Willie Dunn. An offer to Tim Anderson, who has lied to him, who has refused his money, who has humiliated him and ruined his dreams. He is almost at Mark's corner when he sees Jimmy Glenn slapping Mark's face and Willie Dunn pouring water on his head and shouting, 'Wake up, Mark, wake up. It's time to go, let's go to work', and he realises that Mark's ass was saved by the bell.

Rick begins to scream at Mark. Rick begins to smack the ring apron with his open palm. He does not care what Jimmy Glenn thinks. He does not care what Willie Dunn thinks.

'This is the last round,' he yells. 'You gotta get this show on the road. Don't stop. Get on him. Don't stop.'

Mark looks down at him, his swollen hands in the foreign gloves, his heavy feet in the foreign boots, his linebacker's body on the tiny stool. He looks down at Rick Parker and he says, 'Shut the fuck up.'

Al Albert says, 'Shock treatment going on in the Gastineau corner.' The viewers see a replay of the knockdown. Al Albert says, 'What is Gastineau looking at? You can see all the pockets of inexperience. You can see all the panic in the faces of the corner, as they see their dreams and hopes of big dollars going down the drain.'

At the start of round number five Tim almost knocks Mark out with two right hands. Mark starts holding and whining to Marty that Tim has hit him low. He half spits out his gum-shield. He turns his back on Tim's punches.

His nose is red and his body is sore. His fear is great and his will is broken. With ten seconds left, Tim smiles and raises his hands. As the decision is announced, Marty Sammon lifts Tim's arm. A smile passes between them.

Mark sits between Sean O'Grady and Al Albert at the side of the ring with a white towel around his shoulders, a white flag of fucking surrender around his slumping shoulders. He holds a bottle of water.

Al Albert asks Mark if he can collect his thoughts.

Mark says, 'It's pretty hard but I'm not gonna give up. I'm gonna get a new girlfriend. You can't have family problems and perform in the ring, as you know. I'm not blaming it all on that, but I didn't feel right out there at all. I can do better than that and that's why I'm not going to stop'.

Sean O'Grady asks, 'Mark, something else of a factor, you forgot your trunks coming here today, it just seems like everything was against you.'

Mark says, 'I didn't forget my trunks. The trunks were a little bit too big. You and I could have both fit in them.'

Rick Parker circles behind him. He drills Mark with his tiny eyes. He crouches down to hear what Mark is saying, to hear the bullshit that Mark is speaking. The pass around his neck dangles on its string. For a moment, the camera leaves Mark and Rick's face fills the screen, staring out at America. Rick says nothing and picks at the skin on his thumb with his forefinger.

After the fight, after the humiliation, after the fucking nightmare that Mark Gastineau has inflicted upon him on live television, Rick takes a cab downtown, the fare ticking, the

driver singing softly to the late show on the radio, his mind
turning over and over, thinking of Mark fucking shitting
himself up there in the ring. Turning away from Tim
Anderson's punches on national TV. Don King watching. Bob
Arum watching. Dan Duva watching. Watching and laughing.

His forefinger digs at the skin of his thumb, his leg jigs in
the charcoal suit, his fat croc face stares back at him from
the dull glass of the side window.

In his hotel room, the curtains drawn, the air con humming,
Rick crosses at last into his hinterland. He honks back two
fat lines. He scalds his sinuses. His synapses sizzle. He turns
his rage into brilliant ideas. He refocuses himself on the job
in hand. Back in his reverie, back in his dreams, Mark
Gastineau is still six five and still 256. He is still white and
he is still famous. Rick can take his story and spin it again.
In boxing, everyone loses. In boxing, no one is dead.

It's just a fight. It's just a story. It's just a trick.

Tim Anderson sleeps late, tired and happy. He's woken by a
knock on the door. Rick Parker is there, all sweetness and
light.

'It's okay, Doc, it's okay,' he says. 'You beat him good. He
wasn't ready, he didn't have it. But don't you worry. We're
going to make this work. Let's make lemonade, buddy. Let's
make lemonade out of this lemon.'

He pays Tim Anderson $3,000 for beating Mark Gastineau
and they all fly home.

## ii. Fort Lauderdale
*Round and round it goes, round and round with Bert and with
Mark, with Tim and with Tex, because this is how it works, this
is how it's done. Boxers make you and boxers break you, when
you allow them to. Boxers fall in love with the wrong women,
eat the wrong food, take the wrong drugs, hang out in the
wrong places with the wrong people. Then they get in that ring*

*and they fail and they quit, they cut and they bruise, they hurt and they lose, so you bring them back and you build them up, you stitch their cuts and you tape their hands, you stroke their egos and you pay their bills, you hold their hearts and you feed their dreams and you get them back in that ring, that square of pain with blood in its corners, the one place where you cannot go for them.*

*Round and round, to and fro. Every day a new challenge. Every day another day of this reckless life.*

$50 Bert has made almost a million dollars in his fights with Evander Holyfield, Cecil Coffee and Michael Moorer and it's all gone. Fat Rick gets back on the phone to the *Tuesday Night Fights* people and sells them an evening of heavyweight boxing in Fort Lauderdale to be broadcast live on 15 September 1992. Smokin' Bert Cooper will top the bill with ten rounds of action against the tough Californian Rocky Pepeli. The special attraction will feature the return of another fan favourite, Tex Cobb, who takes on Tim Anderson, the man who just spectacularly derailed Mark Gastineau on live television. Mark Gastineau will begin to rebuild his reputation in an undercard bout with rough Rick Hoard. Three big fights, three big storylines from Rick Parker Presents . . . Made for TV, live across America.

Rick smiles. 'See,' he tells the press. 'Don King's not the only one who can do this.'

Fat Rick and Rob Russen set up a night of tune-up bouts in Fort Myers on 11 July. $50 Bert fights David Jaco. Tim Anderson fights Rick Hoard. Mark Gastineau fights Randy Davis. Six hundred people come to the Lee County Civic Centre to watch. Fat Rick takes their money. He gets in the ring and makes the introductions. They boo Mark Gastineau and they cheer Randy Davis. They laugh and they hoot as Mark knocks Randy out in round number one.

'Hey, Mark,' says Rick, 'at least you're wearing the right fucking shorts tonight.'

Tim Anderson versus rough Rick Hoard is a six-round war of ego and attrition, fought out toe to toe. Rick Hoard bangs. Tim bangs back. Neither backs up. In round number three, Rick's forehead cracks Tim's left eyebrow. Tim cuts. In round number five, Tim rocks Rick with a roundhouse right. Rick cuts. Their dark blood mixes together. Their heads and shoulders and faces are covered with it. The judges give Tim a unanimous win. Rick Hoard needs fifteen stitches in the emergency room. Steve Canton, a boxing trainer who runs a gym in Fort Myers, finds Tim Anderson wandering around at ringside talking to his friends with blood still running down his face, so he borrows Bert Cooper's kit and cleans out Tim's eye. He uses a butterfly instead of stitches because Steve understands scar tissue. Tim's cut heals cleanly and never opens again. He finds a new friend in Steve Canton.

$50 Bert comes out smokin' and flattens David Jaco in round number one. David gets up and Bert flattens him again. Referee Brian Garry smiles at Jaco's resilience and lets him carry on. Bert gasses out. From round number four to round number ten, he hangs on and spoils to win a narrow decision.

Fat Rick pays Tim $1,500 for fighting Rick Hoard and offers him $5,000 to fight Tex Cobb.

Jim Murphy gives Tim a hard time about fighting for Rick Parker Presents . . .

'Has he given you any of the $178,000?' Jim asks him.

'No, but if I beat Tex he'll maybe get me another fight with George.'

'Oh yeah,' says Jim, 'Rick's gonna get you another fight with George Foreman? And he might give you another $500,000 if you lose, right? C'mon Tim, wake up buddy. He's conning you. How many times have you been through it with this guy? Don't you realise what's going on?'

Tim nods and smiles, but what Jim doesn't know, because Jim's not in boxing, is that this is how it is, this is how it goes. One day Rick Parker is sending you $50 by Western Union so that you can buy food and a six-pack and the next he is arranging for you to fight Evander Holyfield for the championship of the world. One month you are fighting Frank Lux in Springfield and the next you are fighting George Foreman in Orlando. One day a guy owes you $178,000 and the next he's making you a million dollars. This is how it is. This is how it goes. You get a split eye and butterfly stitches. Your body flecked with the other guy's blood. A thumping head and the adrenalin high. The days of pain as your body heals. Fifteen hundred for your trouble, fifteen hundred and dreams of more.

*Boxing Illustrated* magazine assigns Ken Knox to write about Rick Parker and the Fort Lauderdale card he's putting together for 15 September. Rick gives Ken full access and an instant interview. He tells him: 'I'm a major force in boxing, especially the most lucrative part of it – the heavyweights. From the time I've been in the boxing business, I've been a half-inch away from the windfall factor. I've almost made it. I've heard every writer and media guy laugh at me when I said George Foreman would fight for the heavyweight championship. But he made it even if I didn't. I've had my life threatened on numerous occasions by people who are serious. And Don King has interfered with every fighter I've ever had. Look, Duva, King and Arum know that if Rick Parker gets television, they are in trouble because I could get any fighter in the world . . .'

Fat Rick hires Steve Benson to handle the local promotion. He agrees to pay him $2,000, plus 50 per cent of any sponsorship Steve brings in. He instructs Steve to find him lots of sponsors. He instructs Steve to find him one hundred free hotel rooms. Hurricane Andrew blows through Fort Lauderdale on 24

August. It causes so much damage that businesses close and the hotels . . . the hotels are full of homeless people.

Rob Russen convenes a meeting with Rick. He tells Rick that all of the money from the George Foreman lawsuit and $50 Bert's title fights has been spent. He suggests using the Fort Lauderdale card as a springboard for long-term strategies.

Fat Rick says fuck that. Boxing is not a long-term game. The big score with Mark is what they need. He suggests they take a case full of money on a plane to Mexico and buy a ranking for Mark from the WBC.

Tim lets his eye heal up after the Rick Hoard fight. He eats clean. He trains hard. He keeps his weight up. He knows he can beat Tex Cobb. Tex is tough but Tex is old. He hasn't fought for three and a half years. He can beat Tex Cobb and get himself right back in the picture. He runs on the beach and on the boulevards and he lets his mind reach.

With four days to go, Tex Cobb is sparring with Rick Hoard when rough Rick slips and sprains his knee. Rick gets a knee brace and carries on training. Tex develops a chest pain. He carries on training.

With three days to go, Fat Rick calls a press conference. Tex makes some jokes about his mental stability. Everyone laughs. Rick calls Tex Cobb 'the baddest man on the planet'. Everyone laughs. Rick says he'll personally fight Don King in the ring, on the street or wherever Don chooses. Everyone laughs again. Rick calls Bert Cooper 'the baddest man on the planet'. Everyone laughs some more.

With a day to go, Tex sees doctor Anthony Aquino, a North Lauderdale chiropractor. Doctor Aquino diagnoses severe pain and swelling at the second and third contracostal region of the chest, severe left chest discomfort on inhalation and

pain in the left lower anterior ribcage. Dr Aquino advises Tex
to see a medical doctor. He writes a letter stating that he is
unfit to fight and to refrain from training for three weeks. Tex
tells Rick. Rick does not show the letter to the examining
physician. He does not pull Tex out of the fight.

Instead Rick calls Sonny Barch to the Holiday Inn. Sonny
Barch, his sidekick, his can-do man, his crossroader.

Rick says, 'I need you to do me a favour. Tex's shoulder is
hurt. I can't let him fight Doc Anderson. You gotta help me.'

'Rick, Tex could beat Tim with his leg broke.'

'I can't take a chance. I can't have Tim derail me again
like he did with Mark.'

'I don't know, man.'

'Sonny . . .' says Rick, and lets his shadow fall. He lays it
out: Sonny fights Tex and goes easy on him, takes care of his
shoulder, lets Tex knock the ring rust off. Sonny gets $5,000.
Sonny gets five easy fights on Rick's next five cards, all for
good money. Tex gets Sonny a part in the movies.

Tex wins, Rick wins, Sonny wins.

Sonny sighs and says okay.


Rick takes the limo from the Fort Lauderdale Holiday Inn to
the War Memorial Auditorium for the weigh-in. He watches
the road from the window of the car. His temper ticks. His
arrival at the weigh-in spreads unease. His malice is pure
and easily felt. He eyes Don Hazelton on the dais, by the
scales. Don with his rules and with his regulations.

The fighters line up, the nearly-men and the no-hopers,
the noir boxers and the crossroaders, in their sneakers and in
their shorts, in their T-shirts and in their towels. $50 Bert
Cooper hasn't stopped eating since his last fucking fight. He
turns the scale at 233 pounds, his heaviest ever. Rocky
Pepeli weighs five pounds less. Tex Cobb steps on the scale
at 239. Mark Gastineau weighs 255. Rough Rick Hoard is
235, including the knee brace.

Fat Rick waits until Tim Anderson arrives to weigh in, and then he tells him that he can't pay him $5,000 to fight Tex Cobb because he doesn't have the money, and the best he can do is $1,500 and a fight down the bill.

Tim can't believe Rick is doing this to him. Screwing him again. He makes his protest loudly and publicly to Don Hazelton. Don calls his commissioners for a vote on the substitution. He loses by 3-2 and the switch is agreed. Tex Cobb will fight Sonny Barch. Sonny Barch takes to the dais and weighs in at 304 pounds.

Rick Parker wins in this war of words. Rick wins and Tim loses, Tim loses and so does Don fucking Hazelton. Rick smiles and gets back in the limo.

Denis Jones drives Rick from the War Memorial Auditorium to the Holiday Inn. He goes straight to Sonny Barch's room. He says, 'How do you want to do this with Tex?' and Sonny says, 'I'll go two or three rounds and get out. Then I'll get back up and take a little more and go down again. I'll be out after three knockdowns, just like that.'

'Well, Tex has an injured arm, so let's make this quick.'

'I won't hit his shoulder. And remember, he's gonna get me a movie part for this . . .'

Rick just smiles and sends Sonny to speak to Rick Hoard about his fight with Mark. Sonny finds Rick in his hotel room.

Sonny says, 'You know what you need to do tonight, right . . . Parker's gonna give you another thousand dollars if you go into the water, a thousand dollars and a couple of easy wins down the line.'

Rick Hoard says, 'Do you think it's best?' and Sonny says, 'I got trouble if it doesn't happen.'

The War Memorial Auditorium, Tuesday 15 September 1992. Mark Gastineau goes out there looking like a fucking fighter for once, with his hands up high and his head held down. Rick

Hoard comes shuffling out wearing that stupid knee brace, crouching low, because he can't stand up. After twenty seconds of round number one, Rick misses with a right hand and stumbles forwards. Mark's arms wrap around his shoulders and his weight bears down. Rick screams as the ligaments in his knee tear and he flaps around on the floor, broken and distressed. The referee helps him up but his head is spinning and his balance has gone and his face is cold and white and so the ref waves his hands above his head and the fight is over.

Rick Parker watches in his bottle-green suit and bright white shirt, his red and white tie and cowboy boots, his mood as black and depthless as the night-time sea.

Tonight Mark Gastineau has not thrown a punch. Rick Hoard has stolen a win away from him, a proper TV win that people watch and remember, Rick Hoard and that stupid fucking knee brace.

Before these cameras . . .

In front of this crowd . . .

In front of Don fucking Hazelton . . .

Rick Hoard has stolen, Rick Parker thinks, Rick Hoard has stolen and he will not be paid . . . not in cash and not in wins . . . not tonight . . . not for this . . .

Mark and Rick hear the boos and the jeers, the laughs and the hoots, the shit that Rick fucking Hoard has brought down upon them.

With words and with curses . . .

With jokes and with laughter . . .

With Don Hazelton watching on. With Ken Knox watching on. With Al Alberts and Sean O'Grady commentating.

This is how it is. This is how it begins at the War Memorial Auditorium on *Tuesday Night Fights*.

Sonny Barch has fought twice in five years. He's almost as fat as Fat Rick Parker. His record is 19-3. He stands in the ring feeling kind of naked under the hot white lights, despite the boots and the protector and the shorts and the gloves. He watches Tex Cobb step through the ropes, Tex in the white shorts and the white boots, the extremely hairy, expressionless bad guy that the crowd love. The bell sounds and he walks across the ring feeling naked and strange and hits Tex Cobb with a hard straight right hand that backs Tex up and makes him stumble into the ropes. He feels Tex wrap his arms around his waist and spin him around. Sonny goes with the flow and soon they're apart again and he allows Tex to clip him with a right, and another, then a left and another, then a right and another and he dips down to one knee and Billy Connors, the referee, steps in and gives him a count. Sonny looks around and listens to Billy's count and then cuffs Tex with a fast right and a faster left, his big hands in the small gloves, the small gloves that land so easily on Tex Cobb's head. Sonny backs up as Tex bangs him behind the left ear and drops on to his knee again.

Tex rams his shoulder into Sonny's face. Sonny feels two more punches, one left and one right, one on his right cheek, one on his left, each landing with a soft whomp that excites the crowd and Sonny takes a third knee and lets Billy Connors step in and call a halt, so bewildered by the naked, strange feeling that he forgets to go for two or three rounds like he told Fat Rick he would. On the television commentary, Al Alberts says, 'Well, folks, I think we'll have to cleanse ourselves after that one.'

Rick Parker jumps into the ring, clapping his fat hands together. He does not hear Al Alberts talk about cleansing himself. He does not hear Don Hazelton call the fight a travesty. He does not see what Ken Knox is writing in his notebook.

In the featured attraction, Bert Cooper TKOs Rocky Pepeli in round number eight. Sonny Barch is sitting in his dressing

room, still in the black boots and the black shorts, still in the
blue protector, but with the gloves off and the tape cut from
his hands. Don Hazelton knocks on the door. He needs Sonny
to fill a sample bottle for the drug test.

Tex Cobb is sitting in his dressing room in the white shorts
and the white boots. Don Hazelton knocks on the door. He
needs Tex to fill a sample bottle, too. Tex fills his with piss.
Sonny fills his with tap water.

Some hours later, in Rick Parker's expensive room at the
Holiday Inn, with its sea-facing balcony and its view of the
freeway that runs between the hotel and the beach, Rob
Russen is paying the fighters from a briefcase full of cash.

Rick Parker watches them come and go. He removes his
tie, he opens his shirt. He takes off his jacket and removes his
boots. He places his Glock in his silver case. At 1.30 a.m.,
$50 Bert knocks on Rick's door. He's come for his $15,000,
as contracted for beating Rocky Pepeli. Rick looks at Bert
and smiles.

Poor Bert. He never did really get it.

'Look, Bert,' Rick says. 'You've already had it. All those
advances I been giving to you . . . The money I send you. The
clothes I bought you. The training gear. The hotel rooms. You
spent your fifteen thousand already. You were fighting to pay
me off tonight.'

'Bullshit,' says Bert. 'I'm here for my money.'

Fat Rick laughs in his face and walks out on to the
balcony.

$50 Bert is not in the mood for Fat Rick's bullshit. He sees
Rick's silver case left open on the table. The tiny gun, tucked
inside. It almost disappears in Bert's broad palm. He walks
through the lounge and on to the balcony. He points the gun
at Fat Rick Parker.

'If you don't pay me now, I'll kill you, Rick. I'll throw your

body off the balcony. I don't give a shit. Pay up now or you're
a dead man.'

Rick laughs but this isn't funny. The small silver gun
pointed at his head. $50 Bert holding it steady, that particular
look in his narrowed eye. Rick's wheezing breath in and out
like a zipper, his maddened blood rushing in his ears, his
sphincter tightening involuntarily.

'You don't need to do this, Bert. Cool down, man. We're
friends, aren't we? I'll write you a cheque and we'll offset the
expenses next time. How's that?'

Bert keeps the gun trained on Rick as they walk back
inside. Rick takes a pen from the silver case and scribbles
some zeros on to a personal cheque. The air con hums, his
blood rushes, the pen shakes in his big fat hand. Bert puts the
gun down on the table, pockets the money and leaves with a
smile on his face.

Fat Rick shuts the door on $50 Bert and goes to bed.

First thing next morning he calls the bank and stops Bert's
cheque. He draws up a formal complaint for the Fort
Lauderdale police department. He faxes a copy to W. Russell
Carmichael, lawyer to $50 Bert. He tells him that he'll go
through with the complaint if Bert tries any more funny
business.

Fuck you, Bert, you fucking idiot.

Fuck Rick Hoard and fuck Sonny Barch, too. Fuck Al
Alberts and fuck Don Hazelton and fuck Tuesday nights.

These fools and these liars. This life that he loves. These
storms he must sail through.

The same afternoon, Steve Benson shows up at the hotel
wanting his $2,000, $2,000 for getting Rick no free hotel rooms
and no sponsorship for *Tuesday Night Fights*. Steve says that
there were no free hotel rooms because Hurricane Andrew
destroyed half of the houses in Fort Lauderdale. He says that

he got $2,500 in sponsorship from the King Motor Company, he arranged all of the press and all of the publicity, he handled all of the programmes and all of the programme sales and he has earned his money.

Rick tells Steve to get fucked. He tells Steve to collect the cheque from the King Motor Company himself, to keep it, and to stay away from Rick Parker forever, to stay out of the boxing business forever because it's no business for him.

Two hours later, Steve is back with a cheque from the King Motor Company that the bank won't cash, a cheque made payable to Richard L. Parker, a cheque that Steve Benson wants him to initial and hand over.

Rick says, 'I'll endorse this, you piece of shit', and tears the cheque up. He threatens Steve Benson and he threatens Steve Benson's family. He sends Sonny Barch to the King Motor Company to get another cheque, and when they see the look on Sonny Barch's face, they don't argue. Rick takes the money to the bank and forgets all about Steve Benson.

Three weeks later Don fucking Hazelton calls and tells him that Tex Cobb's drug test has come back positive for marijuana and Sonny Barch's drug test has come back positive for cocaine. He is suspending the licences of both fighters for six months. He is fining them $1,500 each. He is revoking Tex's victory and striking it from the record. He is declaring their fight a no-contest.

Rick asks Sonny about the failed drugs test. Sonny looks baffled and says he filled his sample up with water. 'So,' Rick asks, 'how the hell did it come back positive for cocaine?'

'Rick, I have no idea.'

*Boxing Illustrated* magazine publish Ken Knox's feature story on Rick Parker and the Fort Lauderdale card. Ken's piece begins, 'Who is Rick Elvis Parker? And why are people saying such terrible things about him? Is he, as he claims, just an honest guy trying to make a living in and an impact on the sport of professional boxing? Or is he a paranoid ne'er-do-well pulling out all the stops to join the elite of boxing's movers and shakers?'

Does Don King read *Boxing Illustrated*? Do Don King's people? Does Bob Arum read *Boxing Illustrated*? Do Bob Arum's people? Does Dan Duva read *Boxing Illustrated*? Do Dan Duva's people? Does Don Hazelton read *Boxing Illustrated*? Do the Florida State Athletic Commission?

Who is reading those words? Who is saying those terrible things?

This injustice.

Who has found cocaine in a sample bottle filled with tap water? Who wants to take Rick Parker down?

These liars. These crooks.

These storms he must sail through.

# The Poisoning

If you wanted to, you could look at boxing as a separate, strange universe and the heavyweights as a galaxy inside it, with their championship as its sun. Within its orbit some came close enough to the heat and light to sustain their rich and verdant lives. Further away it grew colder, dark and hostile. Out there, you could fixate on the power and glory of the sun so much that it might appear closer than it really was.

Evander Holyfield begins 1992 as the linear heavyweight champion. He beats Larry Holmes and then loses to Riddick Bowe. Riddick Bowe beats Pierre Coetzer in a title eliminator, and then Evander Holyfield. Pierre Coetzer goes to London and gets knocked out by Frank Bruno. Lennox Lewis knocks out Razor Ruddock and gets the WBC version of the title from Riddick Bowe when Riddick refuses to make a mandatory defence and throws the belt into a dustbin instead. Michael Moorer knocks out Billy Wright on the undercard of the Holyfield–Bowe fight. Big George Foreman outpoints Alex Stewart in Las Vegas.

A white American heavyweight named Tommy Morrison knocks out Bobby Quarry, Jerry Halstead, Kimmuel Odum, Art Tucker, Joe Hipp and Marshall Tillman. A white Polish heavyweight called Andrew Golota knocks out Roosevelt Shuler, Joe Jones, Charles Presswood, Joey Christjohn, James Holly, Aaron Brown and Young Joe Louis. A white South African heavyweight named Francois Botha knocks out or beats Ron Ackerson, Marion Wilson, Ron Ackerson again, Ken Jackson, David Martin, Mike Hunter and Russell Rierson. On 19 November, in Oklahoma City, he knocks out Russell Rierson again, Mike Jones and Artie Hooks all on one night, because in Oklahoma City there is no boxing commission and he can do whatever he likes.

This is how the year of 1992 unfolds in heavyweight boxing. Without Rick Parker. Without Rick Parker Presents . . .

Sonny Barch shows up wanting the rest of his money from the Tex Cobb fight. Fat Rick takes a cheque from his case and hands it to Sonny. He tells Sonny to amend the details and present it at the bank. Sonny takes the cheque to the Barnett Bank of Florida. He amends the details just as Rick has told him. He presents the cheque and receives the amount of $3,600. The bank notices that the cheque has been amended. They contact Rick Parker. Fat Rick tells them that Sonny Barch has defrauded him, has defrauded them both. The Barnett Bank of Florida pursue Sonny for the return of the money. The police pursue Sonny for altering the cheque. Ripped off and stitched up, taken for a ride by Fat Rick Parker, with the fucking cops asking him too many questions, Sonny picks up the phone and calls Don Hazelton at the Florida State Athletic Commission.

*2 April 1946, the Memorial Auditorium in Buffalo, Missouri. Round number three of a heavyweight contest between Joltin'*

*Joe Matisi and Dave Mason. Mason has already been down three times when Matisi hits him with a devastating punch that jerks his head back, that has him slumped unmoving in a corner, that kills him less than twenty-four hours later. Don Hazelton is fifteen years old and watches Dave Mason die from his ringside seat. Never forgets how it looked. Never forgets what it meant.*

Sonny begins talking to Don. A phone call here. A phone call there. Don Hazelton reels Sonny in. He offers him a deal. He'll revoke his six-month suspension and quash his fine if Sonny will tell him the truth about the fight with Tex Cobb. Sonny goes off the record. He breaks kayfabe. Rick Parker knows nothing about it when it happens.

Rob Russen resigns from the vice-presidency of Rick Parker Presents . . . by registered letter. The letter reads: 'From February 1991 until now you've gone null and void on those who need you most. You've disappeared into your partying and failed to provide any stable revenue for any of your fighters. You've not burned the bridges behind you, you've exploded them. You have no friends in the business, only enemies who will do nothing to help you or your fighters because you've made them so mad.

'With people feeling like that about you how can you possibly expect to succeed in this business? I can no longer afford the liability of being associated with you. I feel like I've bought a one-way ticket on the *Titanic*. I did well in this business long before I met you. I'll do much better, on my own, without you.'

Fat Rick looks at the letter for a long time. First comes the anger, first comes the rage, rage at this betrayal that lasts for days but behind it comes fear, behind it comes doubt, the fear and the doubt that is always there, that was there in the pool halls and on the doorsteps, that was there in the negotiations with King and the talks with Arum, the doubt and the fear that keeps him calling Rob Russen and begging him to come back.

He calls and he calls, he asks and he begs, he offers him money that he does not have, but Rob just keeps talking about all of the failures at Rick Parker Presents . . . all of the failures and all of the fuck-ups, all of the fighters he brought to the company and who have withered on the vine.

Rob Russen reminds him of Don King's last ever words to him: 'Fuck you, Rick Parker.' He tells him of promoter Cedric Kushner's curse: 'I wouldn't piss on Rick Parker if he was on fire in front of me.'

It is war and it is betrayal. It is over. They will not double-team Don King again. They will not double-team Dan Duva again. Rob will not play good cop to Rick's bad cop, he will not sooth Rick's rage and cool his temper, he will not put his arms around their broken fighters and tell them that Rick does not mean the things he says to them, the terrible, dreadful things that he tells them.

He moves forward as if in a dream. He offers Rick Hoard $1,000 to fight Mark Gastineau again. Rick refuses. He offers the fight to his bodyguard Jack Solloway, but then he changes his mind because Jack is a crazy son of a bitch, and he might knock Mark out for the hell of it. Instead Fat Rick finds a kid named Gary Shull who has never had a professional contest. They fight in Missouri on 16 November. It takes Mark until round number three to hit Gary with anything hard enough for him to go down.

Fat Rick calls Tim Anderson on a Wednesday afternoon, the day before Thanksgiving. Tim and his girl Susan and Jim Murphy and his girl Christina are sitting in the sun. The day is gentle and good.

Jim says, 'Happy holidays, Rick' in a loud voice and they all laugh.

'Look, Tim,' says Fat Rick, ignoring the laughs, ignoring the feeling, 'I have something for you. You ready? You ready to fight Mark Gastineau again?'

'Oh, right,' says Tim. 'I have to take another dive?'

'It's not like that, man.'

'What's it like? I'm gonna get paid this time? I'm gonna get my $178,000?'

'You're gonna get paid good, Tim. Mark's giving me nothing but problems. You're gonna knock him out.'

'I am?'

'You're gonna knock him out, buddy. I need you to do that for me.'

Rick tells Tim about his contract with Mark, a contract that says when Mark loses two fights Rick no longer has to pay his expenses but retains the right to act as his promoter.

Rick offers him flights to and from Oklahoma City where they will fight, money upfront for expenses, a week's accommodation in a good hotel. Rick offers to fly Tim's trainer, Billy Lucci, in from Canada. He offers Tim $3,000 for the fight itself. He says he's putting Tex Cobb on the bill, too.

Tim tells Rick to call him back. He asks Jim's advice.

'This is a set-up. They're gonna burn you, Tim.'

He calls his father and asks his advice.

'It's a set-up, son. Don't go, don't take it.'

Tim takes the fight. He takes it because Mark Gastineau couldn't beat him with a baseball bat. He takes it because he wants his money from Fat Rick. He takes it because he is a boxer. He takes it because he's big and he's strong and he finds it hard to forget it. He takes it because he wants to. He takes it because he can.

Rick forwards him some money and a plane ticket. Tim

promises Jim Murphy that he will not eat around Parker, or drink around Parker, he will not go to Parker's hotel room alone, he will stick with his trainer, he will watch his back and be on his guard. He takes the plane and he is gone.

Fat Rick is driven to Oklahoma City in the black limo by Denis Jones. He checks into the Embassy Suites hotel close to the Myriad Arena where the boxers will fight. It's cold and wet in the Oklahoma winter. A storm is forecast for the night of the show. What he does next he does alone and in secret. Exactly how, only Fat Rick knew and he would never tell. All anyone else could know was that he had come to a state with no boxing commission and that was no accident. Somehow, from contacts somewhere, he procures water spiked with chemical agents of an unknown kind. He makes sure that Tim Anderson's trainer Billy Lucci remains in Canada. He meets with two friends from his past, Pete Susens and Sean Gibbons, whom he enlists to take care of the nuts and bolts: the referees and ring doctors and other essentials. He pays a video cameraman to record the night's boxing and to make him copies of the tapes. Then he watches and he waits, the only man in Oklahoma City who knows the whole of the story.

Tim Anderson arrives a few days before the fight. He does some radio and some local press. Tex Cobb shows up and does what Tex does best, talking things up, creating a buzz. Mark Gastineau signs some autographs and he and Tim trade cheerful insults for the local press. Tim wonders when Billy Lucci is going to finally show up.

In his hotel room at the Embassy Suites on a cold afternoon on the day before the fight, Fat Rick locks the door and closes the curtains and gets out his keyboard and sings the hits. He crosses over into his hinterlands. The great hairpiece bobs above him, his thick fingers hammer the keys, he loses himself as he always has. He sings 'I Just Can't Help Believin' ', he sings 'Sweet Caroline', he sings 'Daydream Believer'.

He sings to kill the hours. He sings to kill the doubts. He sings to drown the whispers.

He sings 'I Am . . . I Said'.

Drowning the hours . . . Drowning the storm . . . singing his songs.

He sings 'Suspicious Minds'.

He sings so loud and hard he doesn't hear the phone ring and ring. At last, a pounding on the door gets his attention. It's time for the weigh-in. It's time to go. Winter and war in Oklahoma City.

It's dark and snowing on the night of 3 December 1992, dark and snowing in Oklahoma City, freezing cold at the Myriad Arena. A teenage boy dies when his sled slides into an oncoming car. A man dies of a heart attack after abandoning his stalled vehicle. A man dies in a multi-car pile up on I-35. Another dies in a car accident on the Will Rogers Turnpike. Three hundred people come through the snow and the sleet to the Myriad Arena to watch Tex Cobb fight Jimmy Taylor and Tim Anderson fight Mark Gastineau.

Tim waits and waits for Billy Lucci but the hours tick by and he does not come. He sits in his dressing room, bright and cold and white, and he warms up alone. Out in the arena Anthony Wade outpoints Oscar Reed and Heath Todd knocks out Ivan Guban. Tim Anderson goes to the ring with his cornerman, and another guy he has never seen before as his second. Steve Thomasson, the referee, is already there, a long-limbed man in big black glasses, popular with the crowd. Minutes pass and there is no sign of Mark. Tim does some shadowboxing to keep a sweat on. The second that Tim has never seen before gives him water, not from a bottle but from a paper cup, a beer cup. It tastes warm and sweet. Five minutes pass, then ten and no Mark. Fifteen minutes pass.

Steve Thomasson darts to and from the dressing rooms. Tim sips the sweet water from the paper cup and dances around in his blue shorts and his black boots with the white socks. Tex Cobb climbs into the ring, takes the microphone and tells stories and jokes to the crowd. Forty minutes later, the music starts up and Mark Gastineau makes his entrance, followed by Rick Parker.

With no TV cameras and no commentators, with no viewers and a tiny crowd, Mark seems loose and relaxed. In round number one Tim is caught by a stiff jab. In round number two, Tim throws some wild shots and falls to the floor. In round number three Mark bull-rushes Tim, shoving him into the ropes and onto his knees. He tries to punch Tim while he is down. Steve Thomasson stops him.

In between rounds Tim sits on his stool with his head bowed, beginning to see strange colours and odd shapes. The second pours more water into his mouth. The cornerman kneels down and wipes the floor at Tim's feet with a big white towel. Tim does not remember round numbers four and five, in which Mark rough-houses him, throws him onto the ropes, slips his punches with ease. He doesn't see the cornerman wiping at the floor in the corner with the white towel between the rounds. He doesn't feel his punch resistance slide away as his muscles loosen and his concentration slips. Instead the strange colours and odd shapes crowd his mind and he fights on instinct. He feels the first urges to vomit and he bites down hard on his gumshield. He sees two referees, he feels three fighters with him in the ring, in front of him, behind him, all around. He tries to move from their phantom punches. He tries to punch them back, but they're just not there.

Halfway through round number six, Mark throws a right hand that catches him high up on the chest near his throat and he stumbles backwards across the width of the ring like a man struck by the hardest punch ever thrown. Crouched in the corner, his hands still up, his chin still down, fighters and referees appear through the colours and shapes and swarm towards him and the punches start again. Mark hits him with a right hook, a real one, and knocks him cold. He falls forwards through the spectrum of colours and lands on his face in the corner of the ring, his arms by his sides, unconscious before he hits the ground and with nothing to break his fall.

Steve Thomasson waves his arms and people crowd around Tim. Fat Rick jumps into the ring and tries to lift Mark up. The ring announcer says, 'At this point I'd like to introduce the promoter of the show . . . In the ring with his fighter, Rick Parker . . .' Someone in the crowd shouts, 'Get a doctor' as Tim remains on the floor in the corner, unconscious for almost five minutes. Doc Chumley, the ringside physician, nurses Tim back into this world, gets him to his feet and then back to his corner, and Doc Chumley and the second that Tim has never seen before get him to the locker room where he lies on a rub-down table and begins to throw up into a big black bin, begins to vomit and doesn't really stop until Doc Chumley digs a needle full of Compazine into him.

Tex Cobb knocks out Jimmy Taylor in round number one. The crowd of three hundred leave the Myriad as a two-day storm takes hold of Oklahoma. Steve Thomasson takes his money, gathers his things and leaves. The fighters get into their cabs and their cars and leave. Rick Parker tells Doc Chumley that Tim Anderson has recovered and returned to his hotel. Doc Chumley takes his money, gathers his things and leaves. Rick Parker finds Denis Jones and rides the big black limo from the Myriad to the Embassy Suites.

In the cold locker room, under the bright strip lights and the two-day storm, beneath the sleeting canopy in downtown Oklahoma City where dead men fight, Tim Anderson lies alone, surrounded by colours and shapes that he does not know, that he has never seen before.

Fat Rick takes the big black limo back to the Embassy Suites. In his warm and cozy hotel room, he begins calling everyone he can think of to tell them that Mark Gastineau has avenged his only defeat. His record stands at 11 and 1 and he is ready to fight George Foreman or anyone else in the tight, bright orbit around the championship of the world.

The bin . . . The big black bin . . . Tim doesn't remember much of the last twenty-four hours, but he remembers the big black bin in the cold dressing room with no one around, the colours from the ring swirling in his head, still in his shorts and still in his boots, still on the cold rub-down table under the white strip lights as hours go by. Head in the bin and back on the table, head in the bin and back on the table, then a voice, the voice of the caretaker who has come to switch off the lights and lock up the Myriad. Then the ambulance with the swirling lights and the hospital room with the sweet warm bed, someone pulling him out of the shorts and the boots . . . an IV in his arm, the strange dreams through a fitful night, the strange dreams and the endless night, the dreams and the night . . .

The next morning the world is still spinning, but Denis Jones swings by early and soon Tim is in the big black limo humming through the snow and the sleet towards the Embassy Suites.

Fat Rick hands him a cheque for $2,000 and not the promised $3,000.

'Where's the rest of the money?'

'Doc, you cost me eight million dollars with the shit you pulled in San Francisco. If you'd done the right thing, none of this would have happened. You go home and you keep your mouth shut about this.'

A TV plays in one corner of Rick's room. Tim sees that it's showing footage of the fight with Mark. He watches himself fall down in the corner of the ring with Steve Thomasson standing over him and waving his arms in the air. He's so spaced out he doesn't realise that the fight wasn't on television. He doesn't remember how he gets home to Florida. All he can recall is the big black bin and the pictures on the television screen, the pictures of him going down in the corner of the ring, down on his face, down on the canvas, beneath the ropes where the dead men go. Oklahoma City, where dead men fight.

One more thing that Tim does not yet know: he will never box again.

Tim Anderson, 27-16-1, forever.

# Trajectories

## i. Tim

Tim arrives back home on 4 December, Erin's birthday. His girlfriend Susan picks him up from the airport and takes him to Jim Murphy's. She and Jim help him up the stairs and into bed. He barely makes it. The room pitches and rolls. He tries to lie still. He wants to puke forever.

He talks to himself, to keep a voice in his head. He tries to recall the fight. It's an elusive thing . . . The television screen in Rick Parker's hotel room replaying his knockout . . . A vision of Rick, standing over him, smiling . . .

For three days and three nights he lies there in his new reality . . . his black reality . . . He tumbles and he falls, down a thousand sets of stairs . . . from the tops of skyscrapers . . . into black holes . . . out of planes . . . through echoing shafts . . . into deep mines . . . into rolling seas . . . into storms . . . into storms . . .

He pukes until he thinks he can't puke any more.

## ii. Rick

He'd thought that Tim was never going to fall. The fight seemed to go on forever. He stalked the ringside, charcoal suit and a new white shirt, shiny shoes and a bright red tie, the towering hair, the Elvis shades, even in the dark of the Myriad Arena. He couldn't sit, couldn't stand still, had to pace as the rounds ticked by.

The poison didn't exactly come with instructions, but the connections were sure of its effect: have him drink it before the fight, wait a while and it should be working by round number three . . . By round number three, he won't be able to piss straight, let alone punch straight. That's what they'd told him.

Up in the ring, they fight. He hears the small gasps of effort and pain, the squeaks of their boots on the mat as they search for purchase, the shouts coming up from the thin winter crowd.

Round number three comes and goes. Rounds numbers four and five come and go,

Rick can't keep still, can't keep his mouth shut . . . Come on, Mark, just fucking hit him, just knock him out, just finish it, because if you don't knock him down he'll fucking fall down, and then there will be trouble, then there will be fights and wars, then the nightmare will begin . . .

In round number six, at last, at long last, Mark knocks him clean across the ring and follows up, with no doubt and no fear. He finishes it and it looks good, it looks real, and there is no more doubt and there is no more fear . . .

Rick jumps into the ring and lifts Mark up. Mark's sweat on his charcoal suit. Doc Chumley bringing Tim back to his senses, the single camera rolling from its podium, the thin winter crowd laughing and talking.

Now he can clear the venue. Now he collects his videotapes of the fight. Now he can have Denis Jones get Tim out of the hospital before they start running tests. Now he can

cut Tim a short cheque and send him back to Florida with
Mark Gastineau's revenge on his record and Rick Parker's
revenge in his blood.

He left Oklahoma to its storm and its dead.

### iii. Tim

Each day he is visibly smaller, little more than muscle and
bone. It's gone so quickly. He can't hold down enough
calories to stop his body cannibalising itself. He has to see a
doctor so Jim somehow gets him down the stairs and into a
car. Every time they take a corner, his head spins and he
begins to vomit. The doctor sends him to a toxicologist. Test
after test comes back negative. The toxicologist tells him that
it's like looking for a needle in a haystack. After two or three
days it is already too late to find any poisons that metabolise
quickly. Others can lie in the blood or the liver for years,
hidden unless looked for by name.

Jim probably knows almost as much about pharmaceuticals
as the doctors because pharmaceutical supplies are his
business. Tim asks him how long the list of substances that
could do this to him might be, but he already knows the answer.
Jim says, 'As long as your arm, Tim. As long as your leg . . .'

In his blood, in his organs, in his bones, in his fingernails,
in his teeth, in his hair, Fat Rick's revenge.

### iv. Rick

Alone in front of the television, he reviews the tape of
Gastineau–Anderson II. A single fixed camera set square
to the ring records the fight in flared, saturated, unreal
colours, the sound condensed and distorted, bouncing from
the walls. Some guy next to the cameraman keeps talking,
his voice rises above the tinny squeals and shouts of the
ringsiders.

Jesus Christ, it looks like it's been filmed by a fucking
blind man.

Mark looks good though, looks how he did on a football field, not self-conscious. Doesn't even know he's on tape. He is free.

Tim sips from his paper cup. The cornerman rubs at the mat with his white towel.

A guy shouts, 'Hey, Steve, I got you ahead . . .'

Steve Thomasson looks at him and waves.

The knock out, when it comes, is chilling. Mark, with all of his new-found certainty, crosses the ring and chops Tim down. Tim falls flat on his face, falls fast with no hands outstretched, unconscious before he hits the ground . . .

He stops the tape. He stores it away. He keeps it secret and he keeps it safe. The tape of a fight that no one will see.

The press buy it. In the sports pages of the *Oklahoman*, under the headline 'Gastineau Drops Doc In 6th Round', Berry Trammel writes, 'Mark Gastineau doesn't yet know enough about boxing to know when an opponent is in trouble. But he's sacked enough NFL quarterbacks to know when someone's going down.

'Gastineau revived a fledgling fight career with a 6th-round knockout of Tim "Doc" Anderson Thursday night at the Myriad, avenging the lone loss of his 14-bout career. Gastineau caught Anderson with a flurry and sent him to the canvas 32 seconds into the final round. Anderson had decisioned Gastineau in June.

'"I'm a rookie in boxing," Gastineau said. "I don't know enough to tell when I'm going to get somebody. But when he went down, it was a victory and it was in Oklahoma. There's no better place."

'The crowd was sparse – approximately 200.'

Rick gets Mark a fight against a knockover called Lupe Guerra in Idaho on a card to be taped for future broadcast by the USA Network. Lupe's won two bouts since 1986, both against a guy called Paul Garner. Mark will not pick up the phone or return Rick's messages. The Lupe Guerra fight is lost.

Rick fires off a furiously written fax to Jimmy Glenn.

'Please be advised that I am finding it increasingly difficult to arrange, promote and co-promote bouts involving Mark and paying him $5,000 per bout vs an absolute "nobody" who cannot spell "f-i-g-h-t". It was extremely unfortunate that Mark's win over Tim Anderson in Oklahoma City was not picked up on the wire services. So, consequently, virtually no one knows that Mark prevailed in dramatic KO fashion over his nemesis, Tim Anderson.

'Therefore, the damage that was done to Mark's career by his embarrassing decision loss to Anderson remains, in the eyes of boxing fans, as being unavenged.

'Furthermore, I am in receipt of information that you are negotiating, or attempting to negotiate, fight opportunities for Mark with other promoters. Also, I am concerned about the fact that I have requested communication with Mark personally on numerous occasions recently and he has yet to return my calls.

'Mark Gastineau would have beaten Lupe Guerra if Mark had just gotten out of prison or the hospital weighing only 120 pounds and dying of AIDS. He would have been paid $5,000 for what would have been a first-round knockout, another win for him, with the knockout being televised and the USA Network playing up the fact that Mark had just knocked out Tim Anderson.

'Please allow me the freedom to perform as Mark's promoter and advise Mark to perform according to my recommendation and I promise you that we will arrive relatively soon at our mutually agreed upon financial windfall destination.'

No one replies to the fax.

## v. Tex

Tex Cobb fights Paul Lewis in Boise, Idaho, and six weeks later fights Mike Smith in Kansas City, Missouri. He knocks out Paul Lewis in round number three and Mike Smith in round number one. Fourteen days after being kayoed by Tex and incurring a mandatory thirty-day suspension, Mike Smith travels to Jefferson City, Missouri, and fights Art 'King Arthur' Jimmerson under the alias Shane Mooney. Although Mike Smith is a black heavyweight, Shane Mooney is the name of a white welterweight who died five months earlier in a car accident. Jimmerson knocks out Smith in round number two. An investigation begins into boxing in Missouri and Oklahoma, where dead men fight.

## vi. Rick

Rick wakes up one day and he's in China with $50 Bert and Muhammad Ali. It starts with a call from a con man called Harold Smith. Harold's real name is Ross Fields. He came to prominence by using Muhammad Ali's name to defraud the Wells Fargo Bank of California of $21,305,000. Harold has done his time and is back in boxing, smoother than ever. He puts together a deal with the Xing Guha Group of Beijing to take a bill behind the bamboo curtain. The event is to be called The Brawl At The Wall. The fight posters carry the line, 'How to make a billion friends in one evening'. The show is going out on state television across China. Ali, who, true to form, has forgiven Harold Smith, is the figurehead and star attraction. The Xing Guha Group are paying him a quarter of a million dollars to appear. Harold begins negotiating with Rick to match $50 Bert with Mike Weaver at the top of a five-bout bill in Beijing. Then Rob Russen pops up because he is still $50 Bert's manager and offers Harold a package deal for the whole card.

So when the heavy jet heaves itself from the runway at LAX, Fat Rick Parker, $50 Bert, Muhammad Ali, Harold

Smith, Rob Russen, Michael Buffer and 155 other fighters, trainers, managers, promoters, officials, referees, judges, bag carriers, actors, singers and ass kissers are on board.

Circulating between them is a list provided by the Xing Guha Group, a list of dos and don'ts, mostly don'ts.

'Do not use the phrase "Red China" or "Red Chinese".

'Do not refer to "commies" or "communists".

'Do not attempt to bring firearms or illegal drugs into the People's Republic of China.'

Rick lay on his bed in room one thousand and something of the Beijing New Century Hotel smiling at the wraps of cocaine in his hand. He'd waltzed through the airport just as he knew he would. The Red Chinese were so busy bowing and scraping and looking open-mouthed at Muhammad Ali they'd waved everyone through on a fucking red carpet. Which was lucky for Rick and luckier for $50 Bert, because Rick had hidden his stash in one of their bags.

Fuck the Red Chinese. What were they gonna do, throw Bert out? The guy is top of the bill on national TV. Anyhow, they want to see what America is all about. Well, here it is, bubba, here's America: outlaws, crossroaders, chancers, fighters, talkers, politicians, idealists, deal-makers, the most generous of heart and the hardest, all sizes, all colours, all shapes . . .

The Chinese watch him, appalled, amazed. Can't look, but can't not look.

Rick Parker can't stop smiling. Everywhere he looks is a famous face. Ali, the trainer Emmanuel Steward of the Kronk gym, Michael Buffer, the HBO ring announcer, Lou Rawls, the soul singer, Gene Hackman, the actor.

Everywhere he looks are the moon faces of the Red Chinese, following him wherever he goes. Each night they return to the opulence of the Beijing New Century Hotel, where Rick gets dressed up and takes the stage with the

Filipino band in the great lounge. He sings Neil. He sings
Elvis. He has everyone eating from his hand – Lou Rawls,
Ali, Gene Hackman, the Red Chinese.

No fear, no doubt, not here, not halfway across the world.
Rick Parker is glad he came. He hasn't made a billion friends
yet, but he's trying.

People are saying that Bert is a 50-50 fighter, but Rick thinks
he can beat Mike Weaver; actually Rick *knows* he can beat
Mike Weaver.

One punch away, baby. The windfall factor. He can feel it.

Mike Weaver's nickname is Hercules. He has the body of
a Greek god, even though he is forty-one years old. He comes
to the ring at the Capital Centre Gymnasium in front of a sell-
out crowd and four hundred million watching on TV. Michael
Buffer waits, microphone in hand. Referee Brian Garry waits.
Bert Cooper waits, in his Smokin' Bert gown and his black
boxing boots. Fat Rick waits in black tuxedo and the surgical
gloves that Brian Garry insists that he wears.

In round numbers one, two and three, Bert produces his pure
and ruinous flow of punches. Mike Weaver and his Hercules
physique somehow survive and then the usual thing happens.
Bert gasses. For the next seven rounds, Mike Weaver out-
works Bert and wins the NBA Heavyweight Championship
on points.

At the airport on the way home, Brian Garry is in the
restrooms washing his hands when he hears snorting and
laughter coming from one of the stalls. He watches the stall
door in the mirror until it opens and Fat Rick comes out with
a smile on his fat face. Rick Parker takes his seat on the
heavy plane, blitzed and snowblind, grinning his way from
sea to shining sea, above the crows, above the ravens, above
the rooks.

His last good time. His last good time.

## vii. Tex and Rick

Unaware that he has just fought a dead man called Shane Mooney, Tex Cobb takes off on his final tear. He knocks out John Warrior in Kansas City, beats Guile Wilkinson on points in St Louis and stops Mike Acklie in Lincoln, Nebraska. His record rises to 42-7-1. The last fight of his career comes in Winston-Salem on 7 June 1993. He TKOs Andre Smiley in round number two of the last bout on a three-fight bill. On the undercard Mark Gastineau knocks out some guy with a name and a record that no one is sure of after a minute and a half of round number one.

At the same time, almost a thousand miles away at the Thomas and Mack Centre in Las Vegas, Rick Parker's long-held dream is about to die. Tommy Morrison is waiting to fight George Foreman for the WBO Championship of the World.

7 June 1993: black versus white, the windfall factor, millions of dollars, all at one time. Tommy fucking Morrison. Not Mark Gastineau. Not Mark Gastineau and not Rick Parker.

George Foreman is big and flabby, he is slow and old. He can't lay a glove on Tommy Morrison over twelve long rounds. Tommy Morrison wins the WBO Championship of the World via unanimous decision.

Rick Parker watches the fight on TV.

Tommy Morrison will go on to lose the title in his next fight to some guy called Michael Bentt. He will then knock out a bunch of other guys and sign a $38.5 million, three-fight deal with Don King, a three-fight deal that Don makes because he understands the value of a white guy who can beat up black guys on TV.

Three hours before the first fight of the contract, Tommy tests positive for the HIV virus. He retires from boxing on the spot. He leaves the building via a side door. His home burns down in an arson attack. He gets married three times. He is arrested for drug and weapons possession. He spends fourteen months in jail.

Tommy Morrison and Don King. Not Mark Gastineau and not Rick Parker.

## viii. Tim

He readjusts to the new margins of his world. Slowly he creeps back into life. He and Jim find a doctor who specialises in the treatment of vertigo. Tim begins a programme of exercises designed to alleviate the worst of the symptoms. He can get downstairs and drive short distances, but his vision is narrow, his movements are pre-planned and precarious. His clothes hang from him. His eyes stand out in his head, his cheekbones jut, his skin is thin and fragile.

The Pure Platinum strip club gives him a job training their Foxy Boxer girls. Three afternoons a week he slides gingerly into the gym at the rear of the club and laughs and jokes with the girls as he shows them gentle jabs and looping hooks, half-speed ducks and slo-mo slips. He tells them he's fought Foreman and Holmes, and they wonder, how . . . how . . .

His nights are giant and endless. They are storms of illness and regret. Nothingness lies beyond them. They are worse than fighting Big George with his stomach hurting badly, worse than fighting Larry Holmes with a broken rib, worse than having his face busted up by a rifle butt in South Africa. They are the sum of his suffering.

He thinks of Rick almost continually. He broods on his life in boxing. He decides to write a book about it, the truth about the fight game. He comes up with a title: *Liars, Cheats, Whores . . . And a Couple of Nice Guys*. He thinks about it some more. He shortens the title to *Liars, Cheats and Whores*. It was an old line of Tex Cobb's: 'The liars are the managers, the cheats are the promoters and the whores are the fighters . . .'

Tim can still hear Tex saying it, following it up with that big laugh, saying, 'You can have that one, buddy. You can have that one for free . . .'

Jim gets Tim a meeting with a lawyer from south Florida named Ellis Rubin. Ellis is famous. Out of his Miami office he's defended thousands of people over a forty-year career. He likes the most outrageous cases, the freakiest people. He took the twists and quirks of their crimes and turned them into complexities, compulsions, motivations, pleas. He got them in front of the newspaper writers and gave them the dirt and the sizzle behind the story. He unlocked their lives for TV reporters, dreamed up tearful interviews and mitigating miseries. He often went *pro bono* on unwinnable causes. He worked best when the only way out was to be way-out.

In 1977 he invented the 'TV Intoxication' defence for a fifteen-year-old killer called Ronny Zamora. In 1991 he invented the 'Nymphomania Defence' for Kathy Willetts. Ellis gave a writer friend of his called Richard Smitten first choice of his cases. Together they were about to publish a book on Willets called *Kathy: A Case of Nymphomania*.

Ellis was a good guy, too. In 1987 he served thirty-seven days for contempt of court because he'd refused to defend a client whom he believed was about to lie on the stand. He pioneered the battered woman defence in Florida. He freed an innocent farm worker who'd served twenty-one years for poisoning seven of his family members. Ellis was a one-off, a one-time-only American lawyer and he loved the sound of Tim Anderson.

Tim tells Ellis the whole story: the death of Joe Derrick, the beating in South Africa, the bribe in San Francisco, the $178,000, the drugs, the girls, the cleaning company kids, the *Tuesday Night Fights*, the trip to Oklahoma. Jim explains the poisoning, he tells Ellis that the skinny, slow-moving guy next to him once fought Foreman and Holmes and that now some mornings he can't make it down the stairs. Tim talks about *Liars, Cheats and Whores*. Ellis feels the synergy. Ellis loves boxing. He loves the idea of bringing Rick Parker to court. He loves the idea of putting Tim Anderson's story on TV. He wants to go after Fat Rick, Doctor Don Chumley and the Myriad Arena. He smells a win. They shake hands on a deal. Ellis Rubin goes to work.

## ix. Don

Don Hazelton starts to take Rick Parker down. In the name of Dave Mason, in memory of his fighting dead, Don takes him down. He disassembles the Fort Lauderdale card. He picks Rick Parker's fairy story apart.

On 20 August 1993 at the Howard Johnson hotel on Collins Avenue in Miami Beach, Steve Benson gives Don Hazelton a sworn statement about his involvement with Rick Parker and the fight card in Fort Lauderdale.

Under Don's questions, Steve lays it out, the truth about him and Rick.

> 'Mr Parker arrived with quite an extensive entourage, several of whom were known to me as prize fighters and/or movie actors . . . Mr Parker was armed with a Glock 17 which he showed me on many occasions.
>
> 'It was obvious that Sonny Barch was completely and totally out of shape, had done no training whatsoever, and to the best of my knowledge was imbibing drugs up to and including fight time . . . I was in Mr Parker's hotel room, at which time marijuana was being smoked by everyone in the room . . . This activity occurred upon their arrival in town and all the way through the fight . . .

    'Mr Cooper, I heard, visited the hotel room and demanded his money. I was told that Mr Parker's firearm was sitting on the table and that Mr Cooper picked up the firearm and possibly pointed it in the direction of Mr Parker and demanded to be paid . . .

    'There were threats made to my physical well-being as well as to the longevity of my life. I received several phone calls from Mr Parker telling me I was "setting fires" and that I would pay for it with my life . . .

    'I subsequently found that I was by no means the first person to be in this position . . .'

Steve Benson sets a fire of his own. Don Hazelton files it away.


## x. Sonny

Sonny was back in Alabama, holed up behind his front door and wondering what the hell to do next. Oh, Rick had really screwed him with that bum cheque. Put the cops on him, too. Dropped Sonny in the shit right up to his ears. Talked him into taking a dive, left him naked in the ring, twisting in the wind.

Don Hazelton's promise rings in his head. His licence back. His fine quashed.

On 26 August 1993, six days after Steve Benson gives his testimony, Sonny Barch crosses the line. He gives a sworn statement to Don Hazelton. It feels good. He tells Don everything he can. And he's not finished yet. He knows as sure as shit that a story like his is worth more than a pat on the back from some fucking uptight boxing commissioner.

Sonny calls *Sports Illustrated* magazine. He gets through to an editor named Steve Robinson. He tells Steve that he's been involved in a fixed fight. He wants to know if he will be paid for his story.

Steve Robinson thinks fast. He tells Sonny that *Sports Illustrated* do not pay for information, but if what he tells them checks out he might receive a fee for a first-person, on-the-record interview. He offers Sonny $1,000 upfront on the condition that Sonny does not talk to any other media outlet for ten days. If his story stands up *Sports Illustrated* will pay him another $14,000 for his first-person account.

Sonny tells Steve the story of the fight with Tex. He tells him all about Fat Rick Parker and Rick Parker Presents . . . He tells Steve that he and Rick Parker took cocaine on the night before the fight. He tells Steve that he has just given a sworn statement about Rick Parker to the Florida State Athletic Commission.

Steve Robinson calls Don Hazelton. Don tells Steve that he watched Barch–Cobb from ringside and that in his opinion, the fight was fixed beyond question.

Steve assigns an investigative reporter called Sonja Steptoe to the story. Sonja meets with Don. Don tells her that Rick Parker has a reputation for corruption. Together they watched the tape of Barch versus Cobb. Don calls Sonny's perform-ance 'one of the worst he's seen'. He says that he spoke to ringside officials who felt that the fight had been arranged. He tells her that Sonny tested positive for cocaine in a post fight drug test, and that Tex tested positive for marijuana. He confirms that he has a sworn and credible statement from Sonny Barch admitting to his dive.

Sonja calls Rob Russen. He tells her that it was common knowledge that Sonny was going to take a bath in the Cobb fight.

She speaks to Tim Anderson. Tim tells her that he was willing to fight Tex for less than the fee he was promised but that he was bumped from the card at the weigh-in.

Sonja Steptoe and a distinguished sports writer called William Nack interview Sonny Barch. He takes them through the Tex Cobb fight punch by punch. He tells them that he is amazed he failed his drug test because he filled his sample bottle with tap water. He tells them that Tex had a shoulder injury. He admits to some criminal charges and convictions. He confirms that he had been arrested for passing bad cheques, has used drugs and had once been accused of rape.

Sonja meets with Fat Rick. He denies everything. He tells her that Sonny is a liar and then he blows his stack. Sonja tries to speak with Tex. She eventually makes contact by phone. Tex tells her that the fight was not fixed. He declines a request for a face-to-face interview.

Four *Sports Illustrated* journalists review the tape of Cobb versus Barch several times. It shows Tex throwing real punches. Their private investigators check out Sonny Barch. They discover that Sonny has a recent criminal charge that he has not told them about, intent to supply controlled substances.

On 22 September 1993, Tim Anderson gives Don Hazelton a sworn statement via telephone. He tells Don about the half a million dollar offer to throw his fight with Mark Gastineau in San Francisco. He tells Don about the trip to Oklahoma, about the colours and the shapes, about how Rick told him he'd been drugged, about the short cheque and the things that he'd seen Rick say and do.

Don thanks Tim and wishes him luck. He turns all of his information over to the Florida Attorney-General's office. Assistant Statewide Prosecutor Jack McLaughlin, a former US Marine and boxer, begins his own investigation. Don tells Tim to expect a call from Jack.

Sonny slips back to Arkansas where he spends his days peeking out of the window and watching the cars cruise by. His heart beats faster at every engine dip, with every foot eased from the accelerator. He no longer sleeps easy. Sometimes, he hardly sleeps at all.

## xi. Rick

The corvid birds fly up from the margins, fly up and circle him, black and huge. The crows and the ravens and the rooks.

29 September 1993. He sits in the half-dark with a magazine open on his lap. It's *Sports Illustrated* magazine, cover dated 4 October 1993, price $2.95. On pages 36 to 40, between a two-page story on Wade Wilson, quarterback of the New Orleans Saints, and a three-page piece on San Francisco Giants slugger Barry Bonds, is a Special Report headlined 'The Fix Was In'. There he is, on the right-hand edge of the spread in a full-colour picture: bottle-green suit and a bright white shirt, Mark Gastineau by his side. Next to it, two black and white shots from the War Memorial Auditorium; Tex Cobb throwing a left hook into Sonny Barch's face, Sonny's blond hair flying upwards with the impact. The other of Tex in victory pose, left arm raised above his head, inscrutable tough-guy expression on his face, classic cowboy Chinese eyes.

Rick begins to read. Oh, Sonny has fucked him over good this time. Sonny the liar. Sonny the cheat. Sonny describes the fixing of Cobb versus Barch. He claims that Rick and Tex visited his hotel room. He claims that Tex 'came in with his head slumped, like a sad puppy'. He claims he promised Tex he'd go down three times, just like that.

Sonny says that Rick has fixed more than a dozen fights, including Hoard versus Gastineau. He says he's given testimony to the Florida State Athletic Commission.

*Sports Illustrated* have dug up Sonny's dumb-ass brother Kevin, too. Kevin says he took a dive against Mark at Rick's behest. Tim Anderson says that he was offered $500,000 to take a dive in San Francisco. Rob Russen says working with Rick Parker has made him a pariah in the world of boxing.

The crows and the ravens in the margins of his life.

He reads and he burns. He has fat tears rolling down his

fat face from behind the limo-glass of his shades. Tears of rage and self-pity. Tears of indignation, cried in a half-dark hotel room.

**Miami Herald**, 6 December 1993
**Section**: Sports, page 2D
**By Steve Wyche**, *Herald* **Sports Reporter**

Remember Rick Parker, the Orlando-based promoter who was skewered by former buddy Sonny Barch in a *Sports Illustrated* article in September, chronicling Parker's alleged fight fixing?

Well, Parker finally has spoken, and in addition to denying all of the allegations, he is singing the blues because his business is suffering.

'The only fallout that I've had is that we've lost deals left and right,' Parker said. 'The phone has stopped ringing.'

Parker, who is being investigated by the Florida Department of Law Enforcement, does not have the clout to command large audiences, prime-time fighters or pay-per-view, even when he isn't in the hot seat.

The *Sports Illustrated* story, which detailed how Barch threw a fight with Tex Cobb on a 1992 card at the Fort Lauderdale War Memorial Auditorium, had several witnesses detailing Parker's operation. After the article was published, two local promoters involved in the organisation of the card denied Parker rigged the Fort Lauderdale bouts.

Parker, although denying fixing fights, said he did make sure his fighters, which include Cobb, Bert Cooper and Mark Gastineau, stood little chance of losing.

'You hope to make a fight that's competitive, but

you also hope to make a fight that your guy will win,' Parker said. 'I don't believe in putting a fighter, every time they fight, in a life-or-death war.

'If Mark Gastineau, Tex Cobb and myself are guilty of fixing a fight, then everybody I've been involved in promoting shows for are all guilty.'

# Rick Parker Gets TV

T hings get so bad they're funny. Even $50 Bert tries to screw him, but he's too dumb to do it properly. He gets a new group of trainers and advisers and enters a heavyweight elimination tournament at a casino in Bay St Louis, Mississippi. Sixteen boxers fight eight three-round bouts, the winners progress to quarter-finals, semis and a final. All the fights on the same night, every fighter guaranteed $20,000, the winner gets a million dollars. Or at least, that's what Bert signs up for. The show runs out of money before it even starts.

Bert shows up weighing 242 pounds. He is supposed to be fighting a guy named Craig Peterson. Craig is almost as fat as Bert.

Rick heads for Bay St Louis and hits town with hours to spare. He goes straight from the airport to the courthouse, gets a temporary restraining order to prevent Bert Cooper from fighting Craig Peterson and takes it to the casino.

Before he'll lift the order, Rick demands his 20 per cent cut of Bert Cooper's gross earnings, his airfare, his limo service, his hotel room, his living expenses and his legal fees.

The promoters agree to everything except the legal fees. Rick calls their bluff, wedges himself into Bert's tiny dressing room and refuses to let Bert out to fight. Craig Peterson climbs into the ring, waits around for twenty minutes and then climbs back out again. Bert Sugar, a veteran boxing man in a fancy hat, stands outside the dressing-room door with a film crew and explains to the TV viewers that Rick Parker is refusing to let Bert take part. $50 Bert comes out of the dressing room and tells Bert Sugar that he wants to fight, but Rick Parker won't let him. The crowd grows restless. Rick waits until the last possible moment and releases Bert.

$50 Bert comes out smoking and laces Craig early on, but in round number two he gasses. The judges give Craig a split decision. Craig is hurt so badly he has to be helped back to his dressing room. He decides that he can't carry on and he withdraws from the tournament. Rick wants Bert reinstated in his place but the casino bosses tell him and Bert to get lost. The whole night is a bust.

On 1 January 1994 his licence to promote in Florida expires and Don Hazelton tells him it will not be renewed. Don flies to Las Vegas to testify in front of a Congressional committee into boxing regulation headed by Senator John McCain. 'There is mid-level corruption, which is sometimes in some areas very pervasive,' says McCain in his public summary of the evidence presented to the committee. 'And Rick 'Elvis' Parker is probably the best example of this kind of thing.'

Rick reads the writing on the wall. He goes back to Houston. He has a second life there. He has another house and another business, more crews of kids selling cleaner. He can't sail through this storm so he drops anchor and tries to ride it out.

Tim Anderson and Ellis Rubin call a press conference in Miami on 4 January, at Ellis Rubin's home. Ellis invites writers from the boxing beat and the legal beat and also his friend Angelo Dundee, legendary trainer of Muhammad Ali, to provide a little superstar frisson. Ellis likes a bit of that. When everyone is ready, he lays out the basis for Tim's lawsuit against Rick Parker.

'What Tim Anderson wants to do is tell the story of the fight game,' says Ellis. 'There are fixed fights. There are drugs. Rick Parker was upset that Anderson had beaten Mark Gastineau in their first fight because he was trying to arrange a match with George Foreman. In their second fight, Tim was given water and began feeling sick. He couldn't see. He was dizzy. He was vomiting. He could hardly stand up. The record will show that a doctor at the time suspected drugs but could not find any.'

Ellis understands the press almost as well as he understands the law. His antenna is tuned to human-interest headlines. The Tim Anderson story has everything. It's like *On The Waterfront* or *The Harder They Fall*; it is a heightened version of the story of almost everyone who's ever gone into a ring.

Ellis gets the story out there. He sets up a deal with a TV show called *Inside Edition*. They bring their cameras to his office to tape an interview with Tim. Ellis is just about to let them in when he gets a call from Mike Wallace at CBS's *60 Minutes*, the biggest news magazine show in America. Mike Wallace makes his pitch while the guys from *Inside Edition* sit outside. *60 Minutes* want to tell Tim's story in Tim's words. It has to be exclusive. Tim agrees. Ellis sends *Inside Edition* away.

*60 Minutes* tell Tim that they need a few days with him alone, without Ellis. They fly him to Tallahassee, where he tapes a long interview with Steve Kroft.

Steve Kroft and CBS begin to investigate Fat Rick. They get ahold of Rob Russen and Rob opens things up for them. He explains how Rick fixes boxing matches. He helps them to find his old friend Derrick 'Starfire' Dukes, Mark Gastineau's first professional opponent. He passes them on to

Sonny Barch. Sonny puts them in touch with his brother Kevin. Don Hazelton agrees to give them an interview. After a couple of months of work they realise that Ellis Rubin is right, this is a story, and they call Rick Parker.

Fat Rick flies up from Houston to tape *60 Minutes*. They were non-specific about what they wanted. He thought he could guess. He couldn't care less. They film him at a gym and in a nightclub, getting in and out of his big, black limo.

They take him to a gym for his interview with Steve Kroft. Steve smiles and shakes his hand, then sits him down and warms him up with some yakka yakka about the boxing business, like he's been in it all his life.

Rick has a line ready and waiting for him, just like Don King.

'I've been one punch away from the Heavyweight Championship of the World. One. Punch. Away. I call it the windfall factor.'

'The windfall factor?'

'Oh yes. The windfall factor. All of your dreams coming true. Millions and millions of dollars, all at one time.'

Rick smiles and Steve smiles back, lapping it up.

Then lots more questions, about Derrick Dukes and Kevin Barch, Sonny Barch and Rob Russen, Tim Anderson and Don Hazelton.

TV questions asked with TV smiles.

What the fuck does Steve Kroft think? That he won't be able to answer them? That Don King wouldn't be able to answer them? That Bob Arum wouldn't be able to answer them? He almost laughs in Steve Kroft's face.

Mike Wallace, producer Rich Bonin and Steve Kroft lock down their story. Tim Anderson and Ellis Rubin are out. Rick Parker and corruption in boxing are in. They research, fact-check and edit with their usual thoroughness. They weave interviews with Rob Russen, Don Hazelton, Sonny Barch, Kevin Barch, Derrick Dukes and Rick Parker in with fight films and footage from John McCain's Congressional hearings into boxing. They produce a fifteen-minute film for broadcast as part of the edition transmitting on 17 April 1994.

17 April 1994: the day that Rick Parker gets TV.

Fat Rick watches *60 Minutes* in a darkened hotel room. His own great head fills the screen before him, changing the colours of the walls to the colours of his suit and the colours of his hair. The room lights up with the televisual version of himself.

He doesn't like it much. This TV version of his life isn't the one he thought he'd lived. This one is a crock. This one is a fit-up. This one is a con.

In his voice of deep chocolate, Steve Kroft tells America, 'Boxing has been called the red-light district of sports, run by a hierarchy of scoundrels. Thirty years ago, Congress dealt boxing's crooks and con men what amounted to a technical knockout, making it a federal crime to fix a prize fight. No one has ever been convicted under that law. But if you think that means fixed fights don't happen, think again . . .'

A smash cut to that fat fuck Sonny Barch wobbling around the ring on *Tuesday Night Fights*.

'Take this fight in Fort Lauderdale, Florida, a fight watched by millions of Americans on the USA Network,' says Steve Kroft's voiceover. 'Randall "Tex" Cobb versus Sonny Barch . . . And if Barch looks a little overweight and out of shape, that's because he is.'

Another jump cut, this time to Don fucking Hazelton saying, 'It was a travesty.'

Steve Kroft: 'It was fixed?'

'Yes.'

Sonny Barch is standing in a gym. Rick has not seen him for almost a year and Sonny looks different, older, quieter.

His hair is shorter than before, his moustache clipped closer.
He wears a blue tracksuit with orange flashes on the shoul-
ers. He looks discomfited. He says, 'It was my job to make
sure these guys got wins.'

'So you were a fixer?' Steve Kroft asks.

'That wasn't what it started out, but that's what it become'.

Don Hazelton calls Rick a con man. Steve Kroft calls him a
professional pool shark. Rob Russen tells America about the
twelve wins Mark Gastineau needed in order to get a fight
with George Foreman. He says that Rick Parker asked him to
fix Mark's first professional victory.

'How long did it last?' Steve Kroft asks.

'About eighteen seconds. Including the ten seconds it
takes to count you out.'

They show the film of Mark kayoing Derrick Dukes.
Derrick goes flying across the ring and lands on his back.

'Totally fixed,' says Derrick Dukes.

Next comes Sonny's dumb-ass brother, Kevin.

'It was easy money for me,' Kevin says. 'I been hit before.
I'm a untrained person. I went in there totally naked.'

Rick's face fades in for one last time. He hears his TV voice,
high and adenoidal, a fat guy's voice, a bad guy's voice: 'This
is a story that is concocted by a vindictive former employee of
mine who was at one time under a boxing contract with this
promoter, who was dismissed from my boxing contract and
dismissed as my friend because he stole from me, okay?'

How the world hears him. How the world sees him.

'Rick,' says Steve Kroft, 'Sonny is not the only person
making these allegations.'

'Really? Who are the other people?'

'Rob Russen.'

'Rob Russen is my former vice-president who is only going
along with the story in attempts to destroy me, okay? He's trying
to steal the boxing services of Bert Cooper and be his promoter.'

'So you're saying, you're innocent?'

'Yes. These people that are making these accusations about fight fixing are a bunch of low-life, scumball pieces of crap. They are liars, thieves, drug addicts or are motivated by greed or their own personal desire for gain. They want to harm me or destroy me for their selfish reasons.'

His own voice is talking to him, high and plaintive, his own face is looking at him as the great red weave dissolves into a shot of Tim Anderson flattening Mark Gastineau in San Francisco. In voiceover, Steve Kroft says: 'Rick Parker's plans for Mark Gastineau were destroyed on June ninth, 1992, when Mark Gastineau stepped into the ring for his tenth professional fight against someone who knew how to fight and wasn't interested in taking a dive.'

The film ends and cuts to Steve back in the studio in his million-dollar suit. He smiles and says thπat Rick will now be investigated by the FBI, and then he smiles again and says goodnight.


Ellis Rubin understands that *60 Minutes* have screwed Tim Anderson over. They've edited him out of his own story. They've shown a ten second clip of him knocking Mark Gastineau down and not even mentioned his name. They have removed all of the heat from his case against Rick and sprayed it in other directions. Tim has been taken in by their bullshit about talking to him alone, about keeping Ellis out of things for a few days. Well, that's what you get for keeping Ellis Rubin out of things. You get screwed. You get fucked. Ellis informs Tim that he can no longer handle his case.

*Orlando Sentinel*, 15 May 1994
**Section:** Sports, Page C1
**By Gerald Shields and Barry Cooper of the *Sentinel* Staff**

The FBI is investigating allegations that an Orlando boxing promoter paid his fighters to intentionally lose bouts. A former business partner of Rick Parker told the *Orlando Sentinel* that he was recently interviewed by FBI agents about Parker's boxing and business practices.

Rob Russen of Sarasota is one of several former associates of Parker who say Parker told fighters to intentionally lose bouts against heavyweight fighters Randall 'Tex' Cobb and former New York Jets pro football player Mark Gastineau.

Russen spoke with FBI agents for ninety minutes in March on his dealings with Parker and is scheduled to meet with them again soon, he said.

'They were looking to expand to see if it fell under the RICO (Racketeer Influenced and Corrupt Organisations) Act,' Russen said. 'They asked me about the Gastineau stuff.'

An FBI spokesman in Orlando would neither confirm nor deny that an investigation on Parker is underway.

Parker could not be reached for comment last week. Telephone calls to his home in Orlando showed that the number was recently disconnected.

In the past Parker has denied that he fixed any fights, saying that the charges were trumped up by Russen and others because of money disputes and because they are jealous of his promoting skill.

'There is no evidence of me making any illegal inducements to any fighter,' Parker told the *Orlando Sentinel* in March. 'There is no evidence because there is no truth to these accusations.'

The flamboyant former Lakeland rock concert promoter has built a small fortune as owner of American Safety Industries, a company that hired door-to-door salesmen to sell household cleaning products.

Tim walks across the parking lot at the Pure Platinum strip club. He's just finished training the Foxy Boxers. The late afternoon drains the sting from the heat. As he dips into the shade of the main building and nears his car, as he passes from sunlight into shadow, four men jump out of nowhere. They wear balaclavas, they hold baseball bats and lead pipes. Tim knows who they are anyway, and he knows why they are here. He tenses himself before the first blow. He gets in a couple of shots of his own, but it's kind of like it was up in the ring in Oklahoma, other men all around him, all landing bombs from angles he cannot see. As he lies on the ground, one of the goons bends over him and shoves a Polaroid in front of his face. It is of Erin, sitting in her chair on the deck at home, her baby daughters playing beside her.

'You better stop talking, Tim,' he says. 'Rick says you better keep your mouth shut because something bad could happen to this little girl. It could happen easy. You think she could get out of a burning house? Drop it, motherfucker. Drop it or you know what's gonna happen.'

Tim gets up on his knees. One of the goons stands behind him and swings his bat and the last thing he hears is the swish of the air as it parts.

Life gets weirder for Sonny Barch. He is tracked by ghosts all the way to Arkansas. He doesn't sleep often. He knows what might be coming.

Two years almost to the day after the fight in Fort Lauderdale, he files an affidavit in a Seattle court recanting his statements to Don Hazelton, *Sports Illustrated* and *60 Minutes*.

The affidavit says: 'Over the past three months or so I have abstained from chronic drug abuse and now realise the damage that my false statements have caused Rick Parker and others.'

Tex Cobb sues *Sports Illustrated* magazine and Time Inc. for $150 million. He says that the story has ruined both his

boxing and acting careers. His lawyer says the suit has nothing to do with Sonny changing his mind.

'You didn't need Mr Barch's statement to tell it wasn't true.'

Fat Rick feels the world turn slightly back his way. He finds
a lawyer of his own and sues *Sports Illustrated* magazine, Sonja
Steptoe, William Nack and Time Inc. for $120 million.


Forty-five years old, fat and fucked, already defeated by
Evander Holyfield and Tommy Morrison, Big George Foreman
gets a title shot against Michael Moorer at the MGM Grand
Garden in Las Vegas on 5 November 1994.

For nine rounds, Michael hands George his ass on a plate.
In round number ten, behind on all of the judges' cards, forty-
five years old, fat and fucked, George finds a short right hand
that lands on Michael's chin.

One punch away.

Michael's bottom lip bursts open. He falls to the canvas
and lands on his back, mouth gaping and filling with blood,
pinpoint eyes detached from a distant brain.

One punch away.

Big George Foreman is the WBA and IBF heavyweight
champion of the world. It has taken him seven years and nine
months.

Forty-five years old, fat and fucked. Champion of the world.

Rick Parker watches the fight on TV. He thinks back to
the Arco Arena, Sacramento, California, 9 March 1987.
George Foreman versus Steve Zouski, Rick Parker versus the
rest of the fucking world. How they'd laughed at Big fat
George and big fat Rick.

Fat Rick, right again.

Right again.

Who's laughing now? Them. Still them . . .


After the attack in the Pure Platinum car park, vertigo
cripples Tim Anderson once more. Exercises cannot keep it

at bay this time. Stairs become impassable. Cars become undrivable. He recedes into himself.

He tries to cling on to the idea of his book and his lawsuit. He hand-writes an outline for *Liars, Cheats and Whores* and gives it to Suzanne Migdall because she knows people in the movie business. He and Jim decide to file suit against Rick by themselves in Oklahoma.

Yet even Jim and Tim's girlfriend Susan cannot reach Tim, cannot touch him, not as they once could.

One day he says to Jim, 'You know I'm a tough guy, right? You know I'm not weak. But I can't take this any more, man.'

Jim knows but he does not give up. He finds more doctors. He finds more toxicologists. He finds chiropractors and faith healers and Reiki practitioners. Then, one day in late November, Tim passes out in the middle of the living room and Jim takes him to the emergency room and refuses to accept no for an answer.

A toxicologist tells them something that they need to know.

'Mr Anderson,' he says, 'I'm very sorry, but it's quite simple. Unless you find out what substances you were poisoned with, you are probably going to die.'

Tim knows he's right, he can feel the heft of its approach. His tiredness is the kind that sleep cannot penetrate. Rick Parker's black gift blossoms in his blood, in his bones, in his cells. It multiplies and expands. He is trapped. He will not die quickly but he cannot live, not this way.

He runs his finger down his short list of choices. There is only one person who knows what was in the water. He knows that Rick will not tell him unless there's something in it for him. The only currency he really understands is money. Tim decides that he will offer Rick $45,000 for an interview in *Liars, Cheats and Whores*. The more he thinks about it, the more he likes the idea. He doesn't really have a book deal or any money, but he has nothing else plausible enough to tell him. He calls Rick's half-sister Diane in Orlando. He explains that he has a deal to write his book, that he has a co-writer named Richard Smitten, a friend of Ellis Rubin's, and that he has $45,000 to give Rick if Rick will give him an interview: 'I wanna talk to him about a few things,' he says. 'I'll put him in the book and we won't be hard on him.'

Diane calls Rick in Houston and tells him about the interview and the $45,000. She explains that Tim has a deadline; they need to get this done in a week or it will go ahead without him. Rick's broke. He needs the money. More than that, he needs boxing. He needs the buzz. He agrees to come. He says he'll call when he's made his arrangements. Diane gives Tim the news and invites him to stay.

Tim decides that he should take a gun to Orlando. Jim concedes that it's probably not a bad idea. They sit in silence. Jim looks at his greatest friend; thin, used, broken.

'You know, you've got to hang in there, Tim. There are still some other things we can do.'

'We've been dealing with this shit for three years, Jim. No one knows how to fix me. And if I don't get this information, then . . .'

Tim tails off and Jim understands. The gun isn't for Tim to use on Rick. It's to use on himself, if Rick gives him no answers.

Jim takes him to the shop, P&D Discount Guns, on West Oakland Park Boulevard. Tim has never even held one before. The first thing he picks up is a tiny little .25. Jim can't believe it. 'If you pull that thing out, he's going to start laughing at you and asking for a light, Tim.'

They look at each other. 'Man,' Jim says, 'there's gotta be some humour in this somewhere', and they stand in the middle of the gun shop and laugh at themselves and the lives that they are living.

Jim finds him a five-shot .38 Special that at least looks like a gun and not a cigarette lighter. Tim weighs it in his hand and fills out the forms. Six days later he returns to the shop and picks up his weapon and fifty rounds of ammunition.

*He goes to Orlando, he meets with Rick, Rick tells him what he needs to know, he goes home and gets well and takes care of Erin and her girls . . . He goes to Orlando to meet with Rick, Rick doesn't show, he goes back home and dies . . . He meets Rick in Orlando. Fat Rick pulls a gun and tells him to get fucked. He goes home and spends the rest of his life looking over his shoulder in car parks . . . He goes to Orlando, he gets into it with Rick, Rick threatens Erin, Tim shoots him . . . He goes to Orlando, he doesn't come home and Erin is left alone at Rick Parker's mercy . . . He meets Rick and his goons in Orlando, things turn nasty when he asks about the poison, Rick sets the goons on him for real this time, Tim manages to kill Rick as they kill him. The end.*

The end.

Around and around it goes. It will not stop. He doesn't sleep in the last twenty-four hours before he leaves Fort Lauderdale. He says goodbye to Susan. She holds him tenderly, wishes him safe and wishes him love. Jim gets him into the car and drives him upstate. They arrange to meet their friend Rick McCallister halfway so that Rick can drive Tim on to Diane's.

At the changeover, Jim Murphy hugs him goodbye. As he does he thinks, 'I'm never going to see this guy alive again'. He understands Tim's suffering. He burns with the injustice of it. He thinks, 'This is just like watching someone die of cancer, only you know that he's got cancer because someone gave it to him, injected it into him deliberately'. He drives home, devastated.

Rick McCallister lends Tim his tape recorder for the interview with Rick. He drops him at Diane's place. Diane watches this stumbling bag of bones get out of the car and for a split second thinks, 'Who the hell is that?'

Tim has not seen Diane for five years. He realises how much

he's missed her. Diane is smart and good-hearted. She has a clear-eyed view of her brother. She had watched him hate every woman in his life. She had seen him respond to the jerks and assholes in the cleaning business and the boxing game by becoming a bigger jerk and a bigger asshole than any of them. She had laughed and marvelled when his strange genius had manifested itself; she had been on the wrong end of his great excesses. She had seen him compounded by drugs and magnified by drink and she had dealt with the flotsam and jetsam that washed up in his wake.

She knows him. She knows him.

'I've thought about getting even with him,' Tim tells her. 'I'm not going to lie to you. I know about your brother. I got a hell of a lot of resentment built up inside me. Two years' worth.'

'I bet you do. It's only normal, Tim.'

'I've really thought about killing him, because of Erin, you know.'

'It's not worth it, though. You don't want to do that.'

'I know. But I thought about it.'

Diane tells Tim the story of Rick's last two years. He's lost his money, he's living in Houston with a woman called Theresa, he has kids with her and more on the way, he doesn't want Holly and Chris to know where he is but she has told them anyway because Chris has the right to see his dad.

'You and Rick were friends for a long time,' she says. 'I think if you're nice to him, he might tell you exactly what they gave you.'

Rick calls two days later.

In Diane's spare room, Tim composes a letter. It fills one side of an A4 page. He writes as slowly and neatly as he can, but his hand betrays him. His letters slope left and then right. Block capitals mix with looping cursives. By the time he finishes, he's covered the page. He reads it back:

'I am dying. Liver and kidneys are poisoned from the

drugs, poison I was given in the second Mark Gas fight on Dec 3, 1992. I am giving my life up to kill Rick. Rick Parker is responsible for the drugs and the poison I was given. Sean Gibbons told me I cost Parker 8 million dollars for not losing (taking a dive) against Mark Gas and blowing the Mark Gas and George Foreman fight. An eye for an eye, a tooth for a tooth, a foot for a foot and a life for a life! Diane, Rick's sister, knows the story, and also Jim Murphy. Diane, you are the one who could help other fighters not end up like me and that is my dream. I am sorry, Diane, for how this ended, I love you and I am counting on you . . .'

He signs it Tim 'Doc' Anderson. He sees a tiny space remaining in the bottom left-hand corner and on a whim he writes, 'I'll be back!' in big letters. He tucks the letter inside his Bible and puts the Bible inside his gym bag.

He pulls out some yellow index cards and begins writing notes to his family.

To his father and his partner, Holly: 'Talk to Jim about how bad it really was. I love you. Please forgive me. I was dying. There will be money from my book. The first $15,000 to Fred. The rest to Erin and you. Also Tom and Darrin. There is peace. I want to be cremated.'

To Susan: 'Please forgive me. The biggest mistake I ever made was not believing in us from the beginning.

'I love you!

'Talk to Jim. I am finally at peace. I am so proud of you. I will be with you if possible.'

To Erin, her husband, Adam, and their girls, Kailey and Paige: 'I love you. Forgive me and be good to each other. Stay in touch with Jim.'

Then his brothers. On one side of the card for Tommy and Darrin was a drawing of a tomato in a hospital bed, a thermometer poking from its mouth. Above it, he writes, 'I've been sick'. He divides the other side in half. On the left, to Tommy: 'Tom, take care of your family. Forgive me. I love you.' On the right, to Darrin: 'I am sorry about what happened a couple of years ago with your friend. I love you. Take care of your family. Forgive me.'

He takes out one more card and addresses it to Rick McCallister and Diane. Underneath their names, he writes: 'Read this if anything happens to me'. On the reverse he writes: 'Rick and Diane, 4/26/95. I want Diane to tell you about her time with me and Rick during our five years together. Diane has more insight than anyone. I want Diane to be part of the book, movie and TV shows. I want things to be run by Jim, Diane and you Rick.'

He places the cards in his gym bag in a small stack and puts down his pen.

The last of the sunlight in him goes out. His world has narrowed down to this: Rick is coming, and he is ready. In Diane's bathroom he changes into a black and white jogging suit. He takes the box of ammunition from his gym bag and counts out five bullets. He takes the gun from the bag and fills each of the chambers. He tucks the gun into the back of his trousers. He grabs handfuls of bullets and thrusts them down to the bottom of his jacket pocket. He takes Rick McCallister's tape machine, inserts a cassette and puts that in his other pocket. He rinses his face and slicks back his hair. He pulls his Bible from the gym bag and tucks the yellow cards inside it next to the letter. He slips it inside his jacket.

At 5.30 Chris Parker arrives. He's grown up, a young man now, fourteen years old, skinny and tall. He remembers Tim well. They talk about Chris as a little kid, about the good times they'd had at the house in Pelican Bay. Chris says he hasn't seen Rick in two years. Tim tells him a little about the fight in Oklahoma, that he has lived in agony ever since, that Rick has done it to him. He tells Chris about the idea for the book and the $45,000 for his dad.

After a while, they get in Diane's car. Diane takes her purse and a camera. Tim slides his Bible out from under his jacket and hides it in the footwell by his seat. He talks to Chris over his shoulder.

'Diane, I want you to look after this young man. When he's sixteen, buy him a nice car. Give him some money when he needs it.'

Chris Parker thinks, 'Why is he talking as if he won't be here?'

Diane drives them to Lake Buena Vista, past the gift shops and the ticket outlets and the tourist discount stores, on to the quiet avenue with its islands of trees. The Embassy Suites stands at the end of its block, the humming interstate at its back. Diane parks and the three of them walk out of the lot and up the curving driveway, through the doors and past reception, through the cool atrium with its dipping palms, past the bar and past the pool, up the stairs and on to the landing. They knock on the door of room 250. Through the glass panel they watch as Fat Rick Parker walks towards them and slips the catch from the lock.

*All of this had happened. But it was not his fault. He hadn't caused it. The World had. He had not done it. It had been done to him, done to him by Don King and Dan Duva, Steve Kroft and Don Hazelton, Tim Anderson and Mark Gastineau, Rob Russen and Steve Benson. And more. And others.*

*It wasn't him, it was them. It was them. They did it all.*

The call from Diane comes from nowhere. The closed door, now open a crack again. Doc Anderson and his fucking book! *Liars, Cheats and Whores*. Yeah, right. Great title. Which one are you, Doc?

'Okay', he'd said, 'if he's paying $45,000, I'll talk. But it has to be done right, no crap about fixed fights and all of that bullshit that never happened.'

Instead, he'll tell Tim about the boxing business. This dirty, lovely business he wanted so.

He has an idea of his own, too, an idea for a book. Because if someone is giving Tim Anderson enough money to pay $45,000 for an interview with him, how much might they pay for a book by him? How much might some other publisher pay?

He buys a notepad and some pens and he begins. It comes easily to him. He knows how to talk, so he knows how to write. It just seems to flow. Pretty soon he's filled nine or ten pages.

He arranges to drive up from Houston to Tallahassee and fly from Tallahassee to Orlando. It's cheaper that way. He makes a Dream Vacations reservation at the Embassy Suites in Lake Buena Vista. He gives them the name 'Jim Nelson'. He packs a tote bag with his personal effects: razor, mouthwash, toothbrush, nasal spray. He packs a copy of his civil action against *Sports Illustrated* magazine. He tells Theresa he'll be away for a few days. He straps his gun to his leg in the ankle holster. He has a couple of hundred bucks in his pocket.

The limo trip takes hours. He just makes the plane in Tallahassee. He struts through the airport in Orlando, through the terminal and down to the cab rank, headed for the pawn shop on South Orange Blossom Trail.

Black slacks and red sports coat. A floral shirt and cowboy boots. The great red hairpiece on his head. The boxing glove charm around his neck. The orange cab under the dipping sun. The heavy traffic on I-4 West. The hotel suite with the ticking clock. Time by the pool while he makes some calls. Waiting for Doc and waiting for his money. Waiting for his ticket back into boxing.

28 April 1995, the Embassy Suites, Lake Buena Vista.

Rick Parker, rising again.

Rick Parker, rising.

Rick Parker rising.

# In Room 250

So here he comes, Fat Rick Parker, up on his feet to answer the door. He sees them first through the frosted glass and he feels his luck beginning to change. That forty-five thousand – the windfall factor. He smiles to himself and flips the catch on the handle. It opens with a crunch. Here they are, Diane and Chris and Tim: Chris got older, taller, Tim got thinner, smaller. He swings the door wide and he welcomes them in. They hug and they kiss. They sit down and talk. They laugh and remember. Diane takes out her camera and gets a picture of Rick and Chris. He's glad Diane brought Chris even though he told her not to.

'Jesus,' Tim thinks, as he looks at Rick, 'he's got bigger, bigger and fatter.' He must be nudging 350 pounds.

Diane makes them coffee in the kitchen. Rick takes a writer's tablet from his tote bag and begins to read. Notes from his book, scenes from the life of Richard Lynn Parker. He reads aloud a section about drugs and some cop who demanded protection money; he reads a section about how he met Don King on a plane and got into the boxing business.

When he's done, Tim whispers something in Diane's ear and she takes Chris by the hand and says, 'Chris, let these two men talk their business. We'll take a walk around the hotel.' Rick lets them out.

And now they are alone.

Rick sits down with a hiss of breath and Tim sees the Glock strapped to his leg as his slacks slip and slide up his fat white calves. Tim sits, too, feeling the gun tucked into his waistband behind him.

'How are you,' Rick says.

'I'm not in good shape, Rick' – and it all comes out, not quite as he planned it but what the hell . . .

'You can see how bad I look. I'm dying. The poison, you need to tell me what was in it, man, because I can't live this way.'

Rick says, 'Well, Tim, it's like this: I wanna talk with your publisher. You take me to him. You can help me. We didn't give you much. It was just basically to get you a little dizzy and make you lose the fight.'

'I'm not just a little fucking dizzy, Rick. You gotta understand, this stuff is killing me. I'm not gonna live. I've done nothing for the past two years. I'm sick, I'm throwing up. I can't work, I can't drive. I've seen doctors. They say I'm gonna die unless I find out what was in it.'

Tim takes the tape recorder from the pocket of his jogging suit and sets it running. He says, 'In your book, when do you get to the part about Oklahoma, Rick? Where's the part about the poison?'

Rick says, 'Fuck you, Doc, that's the fight business', and he picks up Tim's tape recorder and throws it into the kitchen. The button pops up and the tape stops running. When he looks up again, he sees the gun come from behind Tim's back.

'There is no book money, Rick. You'll get no money from this book. I just need to know what you put in the water in

Oklahoma because my liver is in a mess. It's over for me. You're my only hope now.'

Tim keeps the gun levelled at Rick. Rick keeps smiling because he knows he's not going to shoot him. Tim knows it too. Not gentle Doc, not this way.

'It's all right, Doc, it's all right. We're gonna get you new doctors. We'll find you the best doctors and they'll help you.'

'No more doctors. I've seen the best. The only thing I can do now is find out what I was poisoned with. If I don't do that I'm going to die.'

'You ain't gonna die, Doc. I don't know what they put in it . . . a little of this, a little of that. I don't remember.'

The last of Tim's hope leaves him. He slackens his grip on the gun and the trigger rolls around his finger so that the barrel points down at the floor. He sits down and places it on the arm of the chair, next to his right hand.

Rick stands before him, fat and red now, fat and red with his exhausting, his unending anger.

'You motherfucker . . . You pull a gun on me? You pull a fucking gun on me? You motherfucker. No one does that to me. You wanna mess with me, Doc? You're supposed to be my friend and you bring a gun to my hotel room? Are you crazy? What, you're gonna shoot me? You better shoot me, Doc, because I could fuck you up for this. I'll fuck you up for this . . . For that stunt you just pulled, your sister Erin is dead.'

Tim's mind wipes clean with Rick's last threat.

He picks up the gun and shoots Rick Parker so many times, he has to reload twice.

Rick lies on the floor, on his back beside the bed. Black slacks and a red sports coat. A floral shirt and tennis shoes. The Elvis glasses, with one lens gone.

The bullets and the gun, the pain and the fear, the rooks and the ravens watching on.

So this was it, here it was at last. Big Tim, big, dumb, loyal Tim, of all the people it might have been.

'Oh, Doc, you stupid . . .' he thinks he says. 'C'mon, buddy . . . c'mon, my old buddy . . . let's make lemonade . . . Let's make lemonade out of this lemon . . .'

He thinks he sees Chris looking at him through the frosted glass by the side of the door. He raises his head and then he lays it down.

The bullets and the gun. The crows and the ravens in the margins of his vision, dust motes in the liquid of his eyes. The deep black skies above him, those dark and stormy heavens.

Rick Parker, falling through them, hurtling down.

Rick Parker, falling.

Rick Parker, falling.

Rick Parker falling.


Tim hears the shrieks and laughs of the nightswimmers in the pool. He puts the gun down on the bed and picks up the phone. He calls 911 and tells them what has happened. He calls Steve Canton in Fort Myers and tells him what has happened. He picks up the gun, organically warm and purring with its smoking breath. He smells its gases, feels its heat. He slips it inside his mouth. He thinks of George and Jacqueline, Erin and the girls, Darrin and Tommy, the last good thought to help him on his way. He pulls the trigger with a strong right hand and he hears no sound and then there is nothing, nothing at all, until his eyes open and he's once more in Room 250 of the Embassy Suites hotel with Fat Rick Parker at his feet and the gun still in his hand, a bullet jammed in its chamber, a voice in his head saying, 'Not you, not now'.


He takes the gun and leaves the room. Along the landing and down the stairs, into the bushes behind the pool. After the cool room 250, the Florida night is turned up full. Tim points the gun at the ground and pulls the trigger. A bullet bites the earth. He puts the gun back in his mouth. He closes his eyes and pulls the trigger. He opens his eyes again. He is still standing in the bushes behind the pool at the Embassy Suites. The jamming gun, the waiting bullet. Not you, not now. He walks past the nightswimmers and then the drinkers at the bar. He sees Diane heading back to the room. He tells her what he has done. She runs to room 250.

He waits outside in the calm, warm night by the peaceful hotel. A fire truck is the first vehicle to arrive. He tries to give the gun to the first man out, but he won't take it. Instead he tells Tim to put it on the seat of the truck, and has a firefighter stand between Tim and the truck until the police arrive. While they wait, Tim tells the firefighter everything he can about him and Fat Rick Parker and the life he has lived. The police arrive and cuff him and he is no longer free.

Chris Parker runs through the hotel towards his even more fatherless future. Through the atrium and its dipping palms, past the bar and past the pool, up the stairs and along the landing, outside the door to room 250. Through the glass panel he sees his father again, on the floor, on his back, his glasses askew and missing a lens.

'That's my dad,' he says and gets through the door and into the room. He sees the blood around his feet. He thinks that he kneels down. He thinks that he puts his arms around his father. He thinks that he sees three bullet holes in his chest. He thinks that he tilts Rick's head and gives him CPR. He thinks and he knows. He knows and he does not want to know. He gets up again and looks at his shirt and it's covered in blood, Rick's thick arterial blood. He's standing in it, surrounded by it, smothered in it. He picks up the tape recorder and a bellboy tells him to put it back down, and then the bellboy gets Chris out of the room because he sees that

Chris isn't actually doing too well right now, and then Vicky Pettys, who's the night manager of the Embassy Suites, shows up and somehow Diane's there as well, and Chris stands with them wearing a shirt that's soaked in blood and he gets angrier and angrier, and when the paramedics show up they think that he might be the shooter because he looks angry enough to have done it, but then they see that he is not, he is not, he's just a kid, just a kid who's covered in blood and standing outside a hotel room while his father lies inside, and he knows but he does not know.

Rick lies on his back with his feet nearest the door, his head pointed towards the interstate that roars behind the Embassy Suites. He does not breathe. He has no pulse. His lips are blue. His skin is pale. He is in a cyanotic state. A paramedic unbuttons his shirt and then cuts the sleeves from it so that he can open it completely. He places sensors on the chest. He removes the Elvis glasses and pulls an oxygen mask over the nose and mouth. He performs heart massage. He sees no sign of life. He begins advanced life support.

Rick is here but Rick is gone. Those who are left see Rick lifted on to the gurney and taken away. Back on the interstate, behind the hotel. Back on the road, back through Orlando, back through the night, under the birds, beneath the clouds. The siren singing, the road thrumming, songs Rick heard, songs Rick sang. I-4 to exit 74, hard on the gas to Sand Lake Road, the great massed form and its unmoving heart.

The cops take Tim and put him in a car. He sees the detective's badge, but he doesn't get his name. He feels the cuffs mark his wrists. He thinks about the bullets and he thinks about the gun, putting it all together in his head. He's calm and he's alive, alive but wanting to be dead, wanting to be dead and planning how to do it, thinking it through. They drive him away from the Embassy Suites, down the driveway and on to the street, into the heat and out of the light, on to the freeway to the Cassidy Building.

Two and a half hours later, he's sitting in a twelve by twelve interview room waiting and thinking when John Linnert comes and lets him out to use the restroom. As they walk down the corridor Linnert tells him that he really can't discuss anything until he's been given his rights. Tim signs the Miranda card, lets them know he's not under the influence of drugs or alcohol and waives the right to have an attorney present.

John Linnert was a patrol cop before he wore plain clothes. He's investigated property crimes, white-collar crimes, robberies, sex crimes, auto thefts, child abuse and homicides. He is here and he is ready. He is thorough and he is patient. He takes Tim Anderson to his office. Tim tells him that he doesn't want a lawyer, he doesn't want a trial, he just wants the death penalty as soon as he can get it. They turn on a tape recorder and Tim talks for two and a half hours, with detective John Linnert flipping over the tapes as they fill up. When it comes to the part about what happened in room 250 of the Embassy Suites, Tim knows exactly what he has to say. He answers John Linnert's questions. He talks and talks into the tape and into the night, long into the night, letting his words do what the jammed bullets wouldn't.

*Police tape recording of Tim Anderson, Orlando 29 April 1995:*
'I had the gun pointed at him. We were talking about Oklahoma. I said, "You were the only one there, Rick. You really set me up to get beat". He said, "You know, Tim, don't go crazy here because anything happens and you know . . . we'll really go after your sister". I'm standing right over him with the gun, he had no chance, he's in the chair, he's three hundred pounds and something . . . nothing he could do. He's a

salesman, he tried to talk me out of it . . .

"'Just tell me the truth, Rick, don't be threatening my family . . . now I have a gun you can't threaten them. That little girl's in a wheelchair" . . .

"'I was never going to do anything to her" . . .

"'Then why did you tell me you knew where she lived?" . . .

"'Well, I knew I could stop you" . . .'

'I shot him in the knee. He fell down. I knew then I wouldn't get him on tape. I thought "I'm gonna take care of him", I shot him a couple more times. He was crying. I'm thinking, "I gotta take care of him, make sure he's dead, and make sure I'm dead too". I shot him a fifth time. I got like about twelve bullets with me and it's a five-shot gun, and he's saying, "You've got to help me", and I'm like, "My God he's still alive". I got more bullets. He rolled over. I went and got . . . I knew I shot him five times, and think all my bullets are done. I had to get new ones. I went over to the sink, trying to pull them out and reload when he was rolling around. It was seeming like there wasn't very much blood. You'd think, you shoot a guy, blood would pour out, it would be over with.

'I dropped a couple of the bullets. I picked them up and filled them all in. I shot him again and again. Maybe eight times. I said, "I better make sure I don't run out, 'cause I got like ten bullets, but one of them's for me". Then the eighth one's locked and I don't know, and I'm like, "What the hell?", and it won't go. So I kind of spun it and shot again and another shot came out. Went into the bedroom and put it in my mouth and it locked again. It was locked and I'm going frantic, I'm going downstairs outside the place and he's still alive . . . I wanted to make sure he was dead first 'cause I didn't want to give him the chance to start lying and stuff.

'He was making noises. And he kept talking, "You gotta get me an ambulance, Tim, you've got to save me, oh my God", and then he started crying and then it was really getting bad and I started feeling really bad. This guy's never going to make it and even after I shot him eight times, I thought, "Oh my God, Diane, you've got to get Erin some protection because if he comes out of this, see . . .'

'I thought, "He's so fat he just won't die . . ."'

# Part Three

# Abyss

Tim Anderson v George Foreman,
21 November 1987 (*courtesy Tim Anderson*)

# Ken Rodriguez and the
# Naked-Eye Universe

## 1999

*[Signals still reach him . . . Remembered curses . . . Fat Rick dead but still talking . . . his curses chasing Sonny Barch through the burning South . . . New Orleans . . . Memphis . . . Arkansas . . . Florida . . . Sonny running . . . on the downslope, on the slide . . . Don Hazelton taking Sonny's licence away . . . Rick's curse . . . Arkansas officials removing his licence to promote . . . Rick's curse . . . His wife leaving . . . Rick's curse . . . the cops on his tail . . . Rick's curse . . . Rick's ghost . . . Rick's avatars still in this world, hunting Sonny . . . Keeping him looking over his shoulder . . . ear on the night-time highway . . . Acts of revenge that have backfired on him . . . confessions and affidavits that can't be undone . . . secrets he has sold for money . . . Sonny Barch, chased by ghosts . . . chased by his past . . . Fat Rick, dead, but still here . . . still talking . . . still talking if you knew how to hear it . . . speaking curses . . . curses just for him . . .]*

Ken Rodriguez had never written about boxing before but he knew he'd found a story when he met Sonny Barch. Ken was working for the *Miami Herald* on the Sports Desk at the time. He got wind of a guy who had once taken a dive for money and was about to make a comeback. It sounded like a piece. The man was Sonny Barch. Sonny was going to fight 'Irish' Tommy Martin on a nine-bout bill at the Davidson Theatre in Pembroke Pines. Ken Rodriguez had never heard of Irish Tommy Martin, or of any of them. It wasn't his world. Sonny seemed like a slippery guy. He drifted in and out of south Florida from his home in New Orleans, never staying anywhere for too long. Ken found the cuttings on Sonny Barch and Tex Cobb and Fort Lauderdale and he followed the trail: *Sports Illustrated*, *60 Minutes*, the death of Rick Parker. The story rose up like smoke. It was like every B-movie he'd ever watched.

When he first met Sonny he was surprised at the size of him. Six feet four, almost 300 pounds, heavy-set, yet always looking over his shoulder, always watching the door. He'd tried to make a comeback before, he said, but he'd been knocked out by Phil Jackson in Nassau, although because it had happened in the Bahamas, no one really knew about it. He felt that the fight with Tommy Martin could be the start of something for him.

Ken and Sonny spent a few hours together. Ken filed his story. It ran on the morning of the fight.

**Miami Herald**, 25 July 1997
**Section**: Sports, page C1
**By Ken Rodriguez, *Herald* Sports Writer**

Paul 'Sonny' Barch cannot talk about the heavy-weight fight he threw five years ago without stopping every few seconds to wonder if it might cost him his life.

'I don't want to end up dead,' he says.

Barch, 6-4 and 292lbs, is running from ghosts – real and imagined people in boxing who hold him responsible for the death of Rick 'Elvis' Parker, a flamboyant Orlando-based promoter fatally shot by heavyweight Tim 'Doc' Anderson in 1995.

'I can't go into detail,' says Barch (19-4), scheduled to fight 'Irish' Tommy Martin at eight tonight at the Jim Davidson Theatre in Pembroke Pines. 'I've been in a lot of turmoil. I don't sleep much these days.'

In the five years since he took a first-round dive against Randall 'Tex' Cobb at Fort Lauderdale's War Memorial Auditorium, Barch has endured one setback after another. He lost his licence to box in Florida, his licence to promote in Arkansas, his marriage, opportunities to box in Nevada and his only recorded fight – a first-round knock out by Phil Jackson in the Bahamas last November.

The worst part, he says is believing he cost Parker his life.

'It's haunting me. If I hadn't talked about it, I think Parker would be alive.'

Now living in New Orleans, Barch is trying to piece his life back together in the same sport that ruined it. He trains, hoping for a title shot or at least a fight against a ranked opponent, and promotes bar-room boxing shows in Louisiana.

'I love the fight business,' he says. 'There's nothing like it.'

Ken went along to the Jim Davidson Theatre in Pembroke Pines to watch Sonny Barch make his comeback. Sonny got TKOed in round number one by Irish Tommy. Ken was no expert on boxing, but it looked to him like Sonny took a dive.

Ken introduced himself to Don Hazelton, who was ringside as usual. Don smiled and said he could tell Ken all about Sonny Barch and Rick Parker. Ken asked him about the fight he'd just seen. Don smiled again and said it looked like a dive to him, too. Ken flew to Tallahassee. Don showed him the sworn statements that Sonny and Tim and Steve Benson had made about Rick. Ken started to broaden things out. He realised that fight fixing was widely suspected but rarely documented. He felt that boxing might be dying because of it. Destroy the body and the head will fall.

He kept in touch with Sonny. It wasn't easy. Sonny was elusive in mind and body, but Ken felt he was coming to understand him. Sonny, he thought, would do anything for money. Sonny was a money guy. Money was Sonny's thing. He'd do whatever he needed to get it. He'd take a fight, take a dive, find a fall guy, be a fall guy. It all came down to the same thing.

Ken Rodriguez discovered that boxing was a naked-eye universe. You could only really believe in the parts you saw for yourself. It had no structure, no permanence. People walked in and walked out at will, and while they were there they did what they liked.

All that the naked-eye universe left behind was history, and there were even two versions of that. There was the official, rose-tinted history of champions and romance and improbably glory, the one that all the writers bought into and perpetuated. Then there was this one, a secret history, a great inversion of the first populated by men like Rick Parker and Sonny Barch. It was this unforgiving and atavistic past that Ken Rodriguez planned to report.

He met Sonny Barch one final time. It was at a roadside diner somewhere outside of Fort Lauderdale. Sonny showed up with a girl that Ken thought might be a runaway. Sonny asked him for $200. Ken said no, so he asked for a hundred.

Ken said no again. Sonny settled for lunch. His life was still chaotic. He was prepared to go on the record as buying a forgotten heavyweight called Mitch Sammons ten or eleven wins. The rest, well, the rest was all too much. There were too many enemies and too many bodies. Sonny slid away and Ken let him go. Sonny never boxed again.

It was a junk culture, a dirty sport, a cosmic joke. Ken arranged and conducted more than sixty interviews over the next two years. He sent registered letters and chased lost causes. He spoke to boxers, promoters, trainers, managers, matchmakers and commissioners. He cold-called dead men and put a flashlight on the shadows. People like Sonny kept telling him to be careful of this guy and that guy, but Ken wasn't one to run.

By the October of 1999 he had the story. From Sonny Barch he watched the ripples spread outwards. Tim Murphy admitted that Fat Rick paid him to take a dive in his fight with Mark Gastineau. Andre Smiley and Mike Smith said that they had thrown fights at the behest of Sean Gibbons, the Oklahoma matchmaker who had helped Rick out with Gastineau–Anderson II. A heavyweight called James Calvin Baker admitted throwing four fights against Eric 'Butterbean' Esch. Richard Davis and Bill Duncan were suspended by State Commissions for throwing fights against Butterbean, too, while a guy called Daryl Becker admitted he'd fought Butterbean under the alias Jack Ramsay and had thrown that fight.

Ken Rodriguez dug into the comeback of George Foreman. In 1988, when Big George kayoed Frank Lux in Anchorage, Alaska, Frank had entered the ring under the pseudonym Frank Williams. Three fights after knocking out Lux, Foreman fought Tony 'The Tongan Torpedo' Fulilangi at the Civic Centre in Marshall, Texas. Tony was semi-retired. He had a bad back and bum leg, but the money was good and Tony knew how to look after himself.

In round number two, George dumped him on his backside with an uppercut and when he'd got up, George did it again with an overhand right. That was enough for Tony. When he saw the next big right headed his way, he ducked underneath it and sat down. Al Alberts was the TV announcer. 'I don't think he connected, but it's being counted as a knockout.' he said.

'I went down just to get the money,' Tony told Ken Rodriguez. 'I went to the airport with a smile on my face.'

Ken asked George Foreman about Tongan Tony. Big George chuckled. 'That happened to me all the time,' he said. 'If they're getting a whupping, it's up to them if they want to carry on.'

**Miami Herald**, 31 October 1997
**Section**: Sports, page C1
**By Ken Rodriguez, Herald Sports Writer**

More than 30 prize fights have been fixed or tainted with fraud over the past 12 years, according to men who have fought, and lost to, George Foreman, Franz Botha, Eric 'Butterbean' Esch and other top-ranked fighters . . .

. . . Widely suspected but rarely documented, fake fights threaten to remove the last shred of credibility that separates boxing from professional wrestling.

'The fix goes to the issue of integrity and trust in the game,' said US Rep. Mike Oxley, R-Ohio, who has sponsored a boxing reform bill aimed at protecting young fighters from unscrupulous promoters. 'Nothing could be more American than believing in a fair fight. And if that is not happening, then the public has every right to lose faith in the sport.'

Sixteen days before Ken Rodriguez's piece on fixed boxing matches appeared in the *Miami Herald*, Tex Cobb won $10.7 million from *Sports Illustrated* magazine. A jury in Nashville, Tennessee, gave it to him. They awarded $8.5 million in compensatory damages and a further $2.2 million in punitive damages for the article about Fat Rick Parker that alleged Tex had colluded with Sonny Barch in fixing the fight in Fort Lauderdale seven years before.

Tex wasn't boxing any more. He was six months short of his fortieth birthday, a veteran of the ring wars: fifty-one fights, forty-three wins, seven defeats and a draw. His line in extremely hairy, expressionless bad guys appeared to be drying up, too.

He had a sleek and brilliant lawyer called George Bochetto. Ranged against them was the might of Time Inc., owners of *Sports Illustrated*. George set about Time Inc. like a dentist probing a bad tooth. He opened fissures. He cleaved gaps. Time Inc. were hurt, then numb.

Their weak point was Sonny Barch. They'd paid him for a start – $15,000 for his story, but they'd dressed it up as a fee for his 'first-person' account. Only it was a first-person account that someone at *Sports Illustrated* had written after talking to Sonny. So it was more like a third-person account. There was more.

Sonny had admitted that he got high with Fat Rick before and after the fight. He had come out with a bizarre statement about the post-fight drug test, about how the sample bottle he'd filled with tap water somehow tested positive for cocaine. And Sonny had not told them about his most recent criminal conviction.

*Sports Illustrated* had got some other details wrong, too. They'd implied that Tex's urine had contained cocaine, which it hadn't. It had contained marijuana. They had not interviewed the fight referee, the ringside officials or the doctor. They had not asked the people they had interviewed whether Tex was aware of the fix. They had been unable to substantiate Sonny's claim that Tex had an injured shoulder. They'd spoken to Tex and he'd told them it was all untrue. They'd spoken to Fat Rick, and he'd told them it was 'ludicrous'. Of the three people alleged to have been in Tex Cobb's hotel room when the fix was arranged, one was a liar, one was dead and one said it didn't happen and one.

Outside the ring, Tex Cobb was culpably human. But in it his courage was provable. His head bore the scars and marks afforded to few men. They had been put there by Larry Holmes and Earnie Shavers, by Ken Norton and Buster Douglas. None of them could knock him down. Only one man ever did.

And yet here were the words of Sonny Barch in *Sports Illustrated* magazine: 'I saw a real fear in those eyes. No question about it. I'd been in enough football games and prize fights and gin-joint brawls to know what fear looks like, and Tex had the look.' Tex was many things, but scared of Sonny Barch wasn't one of them. Those words defamed him. He was right about that.

The jury gave him $10.7 million. *Sports Illustrated* entered an immediate appeal and paid Tex nothing in the meantime.

Tex Cobb was a theoretical millionaire. And so was Sharon Cobb, but Sharon's millions were even more theoretical than Tex's. Tex had left her a few days after he first filed suit against *Sports Illustrated* in 1994. She thought that she knew him, but it turned out she didn't, or, at least, she didn't know all of him.

Their divorce settlement was very clear: Sharon was to receive half of any damages arising from the suit should it succeed. By the time the divorce was finalised, the lawsuit was almost at court.

The *Sports Illustrated* lawyers wanted to put Sharon on the stand. Superficially, she was an extremely credible witness: she was broke and she stood to make a lot of money if Tex won, and yet she was willing to tell what she knew about the fight in Fort Lauderdale, even if it meant she got nothing. But Bochetto would see it differently. George Bochetto would tear her apart. He would see a woman so embittered and vindictive that she would spite herself rather than help her former husband.

She said no. She knew she was right. Other things had happened, things she could tell no one about. The naked-eye universe was a hostile one; its threats were cold and distant. They came down untraceable telephone lines when she was alone. They left her afraid for her life. When she heard the verdict, she told *Sports Illustrated* that she wouldn't accept her half, theoretical or not.

*Sports Illustrated*'s appeal took another two and a half years to come to court. It was argued on 5 December 2001, and the decision was filed two months later, on 30 January 2002. Judges Kennedy, Cole and Moore of the Sixth Circuit ruled that *Sports Illustrated* had not acted with Actual Malice, a pre-requisite in libel cases involving famous people. They might have been negligent in elements of their reporting but they had not shown a reckless disregard for the truth. They had not intentionally avoided learning the truth. It's just that sometimes, the truth was all things to all men. The original award of $10.7 million was set aside. Tex Cobb got nothing.

These were dispatches from the naked-eye universe. They had once formed part of its secret history. Then they became its news. They quantified its existence. Ken Rodriguez spent long days there, ducking in and out, receiving its signals and meeting its aliens. His stories on boxing for the *Miami Herald* were syndicated around the world. He was nominated for a Pulitzer Prize in beat reporting.

Rick Parker was a small, dead star in a distant corner of the naked-eye universe. The last of the light from his implosion was still travelling. While it did, Rick Parker still spoke.

*Miami Herald*, 31 October 1999
**Section**: Focus, page 3L
**By Ken Rodriguez, *Herald* Sports Writer**

Rick Parker wanted to be Don King. Powerful. Intimidating. Enormously wealthy. Those who knew him said he was so sleazy he made King look almost saintly. Former boxers say Parker talked openly about rigging fights.

A brash, blustering Orlando-based promoter, Parker threatened boxing associates with bodily harm, snorted cocaine, ran out on bills, cheated fighters out of money and allegedly poisoned one journeyman who refused to take a dive. Parker's life came to an end in 1995. He was pumped full of bullets by the heavyweight he promoted and possibly poisoned, Tim Anderson.

Four years after his death, the Parker legacy casts a long shadow over the sport – a succession of fixed fights, knockouts choreographed in gyms and hotel suites . . . Parker repeatedly denied fixing fights before he died at 39.

A lust for riches drove Parker to boxing's darkest side, former associates say. Parker likened himself to a rock star and demanded that everyone call him Elvis. Although he weighed more than 300lbs, wore a red wig, large eyeglasses and couldn't sing a lick, Parker carried on like an entertainer. His notorious hotel-room parties began with Parker wailing and striking the wrong keys on his electric piano, and degenerated into drunkenness and cocaine-induced highs. Between parties, Parker plotted to use race as a way to boxing riches. White heavyweights, he believed, could generate big money because fans craved a white champion . . .

'When it came to business, Rick was ruthless,' said Parker's sister, Diane McVay. 'My brother knew how to push people's buttons. Everybody has a breaking point, and Rick found Tim's breaking point and pushed it. Anybody who knew Rick in a business capacity wasn't surprised he got shot.'

# Steve Canton and the
# Mechanics of Fate

## 2005

Steve Canton was cleaning up at his gym on Fowler Street when he met the angel. It was twenty to eight on a winter's evening in Fort Myers. The sun had slipped down, the night was clear and luminous, the last of the fighters had changed and gone home. A man Steve had never seen before walked in through the half-open street door. He was an unremarkable looking fellow, maybe seventy, with snow-white hair, dressed in a windbreaker and jeans. He took in the one-room gym before he spoke.

'I've walked past this place a lot of times,' he said to Steve. 'I've been wanting to come in and take a look.'

'The door's always open,' Steve said. 'We got some good fighters. You a boxing fan?'

'All my life. Probably just like you. How long you been here?'

Steve told him about his life in boxing. He'd been on Fowler Street next to the furniture store for almost ten years. Before that it had been Palm Beach Boulevard and, before that, downtown on Jackson Street. In all it was nearly fifteen years since he'd decided to bring boxing to Fort Myers. The fight game was everything to him; he was suffused with it. There wasn't anyone or anything that happened in the rings and gyms of south Florida that Steve didn't know about. He was a voting member of the International Boxing Hall of Fame. He travelled to conferences and events all over the country. He'd trained fighters like Freeman Barr all the way to big cards and world title shots, but he loved the old fighters best. He wasn't loud like most of the people in boxing. Instead he was a strong and quiet presence. He knew his place and he didn't have to fight for it.

'You remember Ezzard Charles,' the old man asked, and soon they were lost in boxing again. The names of old fighters flew around. They talked about great rounds and big punches, about names and contests long forgotten by most. The old man mentioned Carmen Basilio, Tony DeMarco, Jersey Joe Walcott, Ray Robinson, Gene Fullmer, Dick Tiger, Gene 'Ace' Armstrong and Emile Griffith. Steve said that he'd just had the great Puerto Rican lightweight Carlos Ortiz as his guest at a show he'd put on in Punta Gorda.

The old guy looked at his watch. 'I gotta go,' he said, and walked out of the door.

Steve turned to get his bag and his jacket. Then the old man walked in again. Framed in the dark of the doorway, haloed by the light behind him, he pointed at Steve.

'Oh, by the way,' he said, 'Tim Anderson is going to be free soon.'

He turned around and left for the second time. For a moment, Steve was unable to move. Seconds passed before he chased the old man outside into the parking lot, but when he got there he was gone. Steve stood under the flaring street lamps and realised that he hadn't thought of Tim Anderson in nearly ten years. It was 2 February 2005.

Steve drove home. His house was on a road called Miracle Lane. He called to his wife, Mary Lynn, as soon as he got inside. A couple of minutes later they were in their office with Tim Anderson's picture staring back at them from their computer screen. It was a mugshot from the Florida Department of Corrections website. He was incarcerated at the Hardee Correctional Institution in Bowling Green, an unremarkable town almost equidistant between Orlando and Bradenton.

Steve didn't know whether to be amazed or horrified that Tim was still alive. He looked at the photograph. Tim seemed older, leaner. In the dark boneshadows of his cheeks and the tense draw of his mouth lay the lag of his prison time. The sight of him almost knocked Steve backwards, and Mary Lynn, too.

Tim had a role in their private history. When he had telephoned Steve before he went to meet Rick, and then again minutes after the shooting at the Embassy Suites, Steve and Mary Lynn were courting and living six states apart. She'd been the first person Steve rang. A year later, just as Tim's trial was due to begin, Mary Lynn bought a house in Fort Myers and moved down from Illinois. Soon she was working corners for Steve's fighters and was almost as deep in boxing as he was. Steve told her the Tim Anderson story; how he'd patched up Tim's eye after the fight with Rick Hoard; how Tim would drive over from Fort Lauderdale to hang around at the gym when it was on Jackson Street and train with Steve and his boys; how he'd made those two sad calls. At the shows they attended through 1996 and 1997, mention of his story usually elicited a 'poor Tim'. But gradually, as their new life swept them along and the months passed, talk of Tim slowed down and stopped. Fat Rick was forgotten. On that February night in their office, with Tim's image filling their monitor, they were sobered by the realisation that they had not spoken of him in all that time.

'You know,' said Mary Lynn, 'it's like he's been plucked from the face of the earth by aliens.'

Now here he was once more, real and raw, a bruise, their bruise. Steve scanned down the screen.

Here was Tim's inmate number: 538979.

Here was his height: 6'00.

His weight: 211lbs.

His Birth Date: 11/16/1958.

His Initial Receipt Date: 07/11/1996.

And then:

Offence Date: 04/28/1995.

Offence: 1st Deg Mur/Premeditated.

Sentence Date: 05/16/1996.

Prison Sentence Length: Sentenced to Life (Life Without Parole).

'No . . . That's not right,' Steve said straightaway. 'There was nothing premeditated about it. Tim called me. He wasn't going to meet Parker to kill him, he told me that. He wanted Parker to admit that he'd poisoned him and tell him what with. That was it.'

'Steve you need to write to him.'

Steve looked again at the picture. The eyes with flashbulb pinpoints caught in them. His thin mouth turned down. His expression was unreadable. The Tim he knew was neither obviously present or obviously absent.

*'Oh, by the way, Tim Anderson is going to be free soon.'*

Steve wrote. Within a week, he had a warm letter back. Tim asked him to get on the visitation list. Soon he was driving east down State Road 62, past the wooden houses and the distant farms, through the orange groves and through the scrublands, under the towering mangroves and the splitting palms, making that right into the Hardee Correctional Institution with its white water tanks and its high sentry towers, its three-ply fence and its curling razor wire, its grates and its gates and its Judas holes. Steve

passed through metal detectors and double-thick doors,
through eyeball scanners and body searches, through
holding pens and observation areas, through prison space
and prison time with its bangs and its slams and its bouncing echoes, until he was waved into the institutional
canteen with its strip lights and its immovable tables, with
its inscrutable grey paint job.

And then, after he had been called from his cell, after he
had stripped naked, after his clothing, shoes, mouth and anus
had been searched, after he had dressed again and signed
the book, there he was. There was Doc walking across the
canteen towards him. And it *was* Doc, with his gentle eyes
and his easy smile. Tim 'Doc' Anderson, in his prison blues,
his number on his shirt, his ID on his pocket.

Tim spoke to Steve in a brand new voice. He sounded like
the Godfather. He sounded like a killer. He told Steve the
story of how he got it, how he copped this rasping whisper,
and Steve couldn't help but smile once again at the outrageous life and the outrageous luck of Tim 'Doc' Anderson.

Steve told him about the man on Fowler Street.

'That was the angel I prayed would come to you,' Tim said,
and Steve felt a chill run down his back, from his nape to
his ass.

'You are the only person who knew me before I was
poisoned, and during, and after, and who knew all of the
people that I did, and who knows what goes on in boxing.
That's why you're the person who can help me.'

They sat at the immovable table for almost five hours,
Steve listening and listening to Tim's new voice. By the end
of the visit, Steve knew that he was going to have to do
something.

Tim had a new voice because the old one had been excised
by a surgeon's knife. In 1999, seven years after the poisoning
in Oklahoma City, three years into his sentence, he

developed cancerous nodes on his vocal chords. The surgeon told him, before he successfully removed them, that it was possible the cancer was a residual effect of some kind of toxin in his system. His vocal chords were damaged during the operation, and when he healed up and could speak again, he sounded like Don Corleone. He kind of liked it, or at least he got used to it. Doctors had found a displaced disc in his neck, too. It was the injury caused by the baseball bat in the Pure Platinum car park. He was operated on again, and the bulge was corrected.

Once he had convalesced he knew at last he was well, after more than seven years. His strength came back, as did his certainty. The new voice was a small price to pay. By the time he sat down with Steve, he was back to his fighting weight, and training like a boxer in the prison gym.

Fat Rick's name had gone unspoken for years, but, after the visit to Hardee, Steve Canton began to say it again, at shows and in gyms, to fighters and to ringsiders, to straight talkers and to crossroaders. He spoke of the Oklahoma show, a show no one saw, that no one remembered. A non-televised, non-commission fight, a non-fight, a Rick Parker fight. Steve Canton knew everyone. The word spread.

Months later at the International Boxing Hall of Fame weekend in New York City, a guy approached Steve and handed him a DVD.

'You better not tell anyone you've got this,' he said, 'or we might all end up dead.'

Steve and Mary Lynn watched the DVD in the house on Miracle Lane. It was undoubtedly genuine. It was also undoubtedly the film that Rick Parker had commissioned fourteen years before of the fight between Tim Anderson and Mark Gastineau, the film that Tim had watched play in the corner of a room at the Embassy Suites. It was a realtime-trip. Forgotten voices from a winter's night at the Myriad Arena came through the TV speakers, tinny and condensed, unheard for so long. The fight unspooled before them, three distant figures in the fluorescent ring, framed by darkness.

Some guy standing by the camera kept shouting at the referee. 'Hey, Steve, I got you ahead in this one . . .' The referee waved back. Steve thought he recognised him, but he couldn't be sure.

At the end, after the knockout, with Tim still cold-cocked on the floor, came Fat Rick himself, shockingly alive again.

'In the ring with his fighter,' the MC announced, 'Rick Parker . . .' The screen light flared and bounced from his charcoal suit and his orange hair. Rick Parker, triumphant in his glory. He put his arms around Mark Gastineau and lifted him up. His fighter, his ring, his crowd.

They watched the film again. They tried to figure out why it came with a health warning attached. The reason wasn't obvious yet, but they were sure it was there, if they looked hard enough.

They began a campaign for Tim. Steve put up a 'Free Doc Anderson' petition on his website. He wrote a piece called 'Tim Anderson: Story of an Unfair Trial' and Mary Lynn another, titled 'Taking Care of its Own: The Boxing Community and Tim "Doc" Anderson', that he put up there, too. Mary Lynn and he wrote open letters to the Governor of Florida. A boxing writer and former cop named Bob Mladinich authored a long and detailed story on Tim for a website called The Sweet Science. Mary Lynn contacted Bob and Bob made her a copy of the transcript of Tim's trial that he had been given by George Anderson. It weighed 15 pounds. Mary Lynn began picking through it. It appealed to her meticulous nature. She found oddities and anomalies. She read sections of the testimony aloud to Steve. On page 398:

Houston Perkins, having been duly sworn in was examined and testified as follows:

Direct examination by Mr McClellan:

Q Will you state your name.

A Houston Perkins.

Q Where do you live?

A Oklahoma City, Oklahoma.

Q Your occupation?

A I'm a warehouse manager.

Q Anything else you do besides being a warehouse manager?

A Yes, I'm a professional boxing referee.

Q How long have you been refereeing?

A Twelve years.

Q You hold any special title in Oklahoma as far as refereeing?

A Currently, I'm the head referee, official.

Q How many fights you refereed?

A Over a thousand.

Q You were refereeing back in '92?

A Yes sir.

Q Did you referee the Mark Gastineau/Timothy Anderson fight in December of that year?

A Yes sir.

Steve Canton, who knew everyone, who remembered everything, who was lost in boxing, looked up and said, 'No, Mary Lynn, that can't be right. Houston Perkins is a boxer, not a referee.'

In his records and in his Rolodex Steve found the answers. Houston Perkins was a super-featherweight from Oklahoma City. Between 2 May 1992 and 10 April 1997, he fought eight times and lost them all. He was knocked out in the first round on seven occasions. He boxed just once in Oklahoma City, against Rodrigo Cerda, on 10 December 1992, seven days after Tim Anderson fought Mark Gastineau at the Myriad Arena.

Steve recalled a fight that Perkins had in St Louis on a card promoted by his friend Jim Howell. He got on the phone to Jim, who described Houston Perkins as 'kind of small' and with 'a full head of hair'.

He looked at the fight film again with Mary Lynn. Through the flaring pixels, across the dead years, they picked out the white-shirted referee. A tall man with long and loose limbs and a head like a pool ball looked back at them.

They ran the tape again. They made out the briefest of introductions to the crowd: 'Your referee, Steve "S-S" Thomasson.'

Steve flipped through the Rolodex again. He found his friend Joe Miller, who had been appointed as the first commissioner of boxing for the State of Oklahoma when they finally got it in their heads to start one up in 1995. Joe gave him Steve Thomasson's phone number. Steve called. As their conversation began, he remembered how he knew Steve Thomasson.

'Hey,' he said. 'You remember three shows I put on down in Oklahoma around eighty, eighty-one? Tough-guy shows. I think you refereed for me.'

'I think I did,' said Steve Thomasson.

'Well, it's good to talk to you again. Listen, I wondered if you remembered something else, too. You remember refereeing Tim Anderson and Mark Gastineau at the Myriad?'

'Yeah, Joe Miller asked me that. I don't think I did. I think it was Houston Perkins.'

'Steve, I'm going to send you the fight tape. Will you take a look at it for me and see if it's you?'

'Sure I will, no problem.'

Steve sent the tape. A few days later he called.

Steve Thomasson said, 'It's me. It's definitely me . . .'

# The Trial of Tim Anderson

## 1995

[*A man walks into a hotel room with a gun. He shoots the guy inside and walks out again. He spends two hours telling the cops how and why he did it. He asks them for the death penalty . . .*

*A man with a grudge lures another man to a hotel room with a promise of money. When he gets there, he shoots him. He calls the cops and turns himself in. He tells them that he is dying and makes a full, taped confession . . .*

*A man meets a former friend at a hotel because he needs some information that he can't get anywhere else. He tries to shake the guy up by pointing a gun at him. His mind goes blank and the next thing he knows, his former friend is lying dead at his feet . . .*

*A sick man meets a sociopath who has ruined his life. He buys a gun. He writes a series of goodbye letters to his family. Overcome by fear and paranoia, he pulls the trigger, then he tries to kill himself. The trauma is so great, he cannot remember the details . . .*

*Two men walk into a hotel room. One man walks out. One cannot say what has happened and one cannot remember . . .*

*Which of these was true?*
*None of them were true.*
*All of them were true.]*

Rick Parker had one story left to tell. It was marked on his body. He was taken from the emergency room on Sand Lake Road to the Orange County Medical Examiner's Facility on Lucerne Terrace to tell it. They laid him on the slab, shaved and pale. He had been dead for twenty-five hours. The wounds on him, randomly placed from shin to sternum, were the size of small coins, and were the almost the same red colour as his hair. There were twenty of them. Some marked entrances and some marked exits. There were two small tubes sewn into his chest, part of the efforts to resuscitate him. There were slight patches of discoloration near some of the wound coins, but these had occurred post-mortem. He looked somehow undamaged, just enormously still. He was photographed 164 times, in sections from head to toe and front to back, at full length and in extreme close up.

Fat Rick really didn't need that. He just wasn't in shape for it.

Dr Thomas Hegert, the Chief Medical Examiner of the Ninth District, began his autopsy on 29 April 1995 and completed it the following day. His report ran to twenty-one pages. He'd been writing reports like it for forty years. Unexpected death had been his life's work. Rick Parker was in experienced hands.

And now those hands prised him apart.

OFFICE OF THE MEDICAL EXAMINER
DISTRICT NINE
1401 Lucerne Terrace
Orlando, Florida 32806-2014

REPORT OF AUTOPSY

DECEDENT: Richard L Parker CASE NUMBER:
NEH 529 - 95
MANNER OF DEATH: Homicide IDENTIFIED BY:
Fingerprint comparison
AGE: 39 Years                    HEIGHT: 74 inches
SEX: Male                        WEIGHT: 344lbs
RACE: White      DATE OF DEATH: 28 April 1995

DATE/TIME OF AUTOPSY: April 29 and 30 1995 at
11.00am
PERFORMED BY: Thomas F Hegert, M.D., Chief
Medical Examiner

PROBABLE CAUSE OF DEATH: Massive hemothorax and hemoperitoneum due to penetrating
injuries of liver and diaphragms due to multiple
gunshot wounds to trunk.

### FINAL ANATOMIC DIAGNOSIS

1. Multiple (20) firearm injuries of trunk and
   extremities
2. Penetrating injuries of liver, diaphragms,
   intestines and soft tissue secondary to no. 1
3. Massive hemothorax and hemoperitoneum
   secondary to no. 1 and no. 2
4. Marked obesity
5. Hepatomegaly, 2425 grams, with multiple
   lacerations
6. Splenomegaly, 400 grams, congestion.

### TOXICOLOGIC ANALYSIS

Toxicology studies performed on postmortem blood
reveal no evidence of toxic substances. Blood
alcohol determination reveals an alcohol level of
0.02gm%

The hands of Dr Hegert gave Rick Parker the voice to tell what he could. Once Hegert had made his Y-shaped incision and tracked the paths of all of the bullets, recovered those still inside and marked them with a roman numeral indicating the sequence of their removal, once he had placed them in individual glass vials and sealed each one, once he had compared them to the holes in Rick Parker's clothes – black slacks and a red sports coat, a cowboy shirt and Nike shoes – once he had removed the organ tree and weighed its fruit, once he had taken swabs and samples of blood and spinal fluid, nasal discharge, bile and ocular fluid, once he had dissected the neck and examined the throat, once he had pulled some hair from the head and yanked out a section of the frazzled hairpiece, once he had reflected the scalp and removed and sectioned the brain, once he had analysed microscopically sections of the heart, the coronary arteries, the lungs, the liver, the pancreas, the kidneys, the adrenals and the thyroid, once he had ordered toxicology studies of the bloods and fluids, once he had, as was his duty, replaced the body parts and restored the body as far as he could, once his hands were washed and clean and still, Rick Parker, in this world, had nothing more to say.

Bill McClellan was watching TV when he first heard of Tim Anderson. He liked boxing, so he'd sat up and taken notice when Tim's face came on the local news. He wondered what would make someone like Tim shoot a man to death in a hotel room. Bill was a public defender. He'd been in the DA's office for five years. He was in charge of the county court, so he could pretty much choose what cases he wanted to get involved with. Bill's office sent an investigator out to meet Tim, to find out if he had representation. Word came back that it was Ellis Rubin. They knew Ellis. They knew the kind of cases that Ellis liked, and this sounded like Ellis's kind of case, televisual somehow. Like a crime show episode or an old-time B-movie.

Ellis had driven up to Orlando from Miami and spent five hours telling Tim why he should forget about the *60 Minutes* business and let Ellis take him on again because he was pretty sure he could get Tim off.

Tim agreed, so Ellis was representing him when he was indicted on a charge of murder in the first degree. Ellis told the press outside the courthouse that he'd be asking for psychiatric testing. He reminded them that Rick Parker was under investigation by the FBI at the time of his death. 'This will be a continuation of the federal investigation into corruption in boxing,' Ellis said, 'and I plan to use my subpoena powers and let the jury hear the whole sordid mess.'

But before Ellis's subpoena powers could kick in, the Ellis situation seemed to change, as Ellis situations sometimes did. He said he didn't have the money or the resources to continue, and he was gone once again.

Bill McClellan went to the Orange County Jail to meet with Tim Anderson. He took Patricia Cashman, who was head of the Major Crimes Division. She'd been a public defender for eleven years. For the past eight, she'd worked death penalty cases. State-sponsored death had become her subject, her speciality.

The State wanted to kill Tim Anderson. And Tim Anderson wanted the State to kill him, too. He still lived with the poison. He had constant headaches and vertigo. He carried the weight of everything that had happened and everything he had done.

Patricia and Bill began to talk to him. He told them the story of him and Fat Rick, of how he ended up in the Orange County Jail. He told them everything. Patricia and Bill thought he was truthful, honest and sincere. They were together, lawyers and client.

Patricia had a rule that she was always giving Bill, that you must never become your client's friend. She met two to three people a week who'd been charged with murder. Some had done it and some hadn't. Sooner or later, however much you liked them, you had to watch them go to jail. You had to watch them die. It was much harder to do these things if you were their friend. You needed a rule, for your sake as much as theirs. That's what she was always telling Bill. Bill knew he'd blown it within a few hours of meeting Tim. Trish blew it too. There was something about Tim Anderson, a strange combination of naivety and strength, of honour and malleability, that drew them to him. The way he told his story made it impossible not to befriend him, to want the best for him. But the story he told them was a hard story to hear.

The State appointed a strong litigator called Dorothy Sedgwick to the case. Dorothy knew Tim Anderson was guilty of murder. People like Tim Anderson only ever got off in the movies. In Orange County, they did not. In Orange County, people like Tim Anderson went to jail, they were sentenced to death, they were executed. There were no last-minute witnesses waiting to take the stand on their behalf. No tearful reunions on courthouse steps waiting for them.

Patricia and Bill hired an investigator named Grace Villazon. Grace was a specialist in homicide and death penalty cases. Together they went to work. The focus of their strategy was to remove the death penalty as a possible sentence before the case came to trial. Getting death off the table was never easy; getting this death off the table was more difficult than usual. Tim had done a pretty good job of getting death on the table from the moment he bought the gun and used it to shoot Rick Parker.

His life was a life of locked rooms now. Inside them, day and night were regulated by strip lights. He woke up when they came on and slept when they went off. His nights had become nights of tideless calm; cool seas of dreamless sleep. The unyielding routine gave his life its form, so he simply let go and sank in. His hair grew down to his shoulders. He thought about shaving his head. He had the pale and pasty pallor of jail, all bad food and no sun.

Each week, Bill and Patricia would come to the prison. The guards brought Tim up from the cells to meet them. In his handcuffs and his leg irons they walked him slowly to the front of the jailhouse, along the ringing corridors, past more small, grey rooms and into another near the entrance to the prison that they kept for the lawyers to visit clients. The room was at the front because they didn't want the lawyers coming too far in. They didn't want anyone coming too far in. Tim would sit down and they'd undo his cuffs and Bill would tell him who they'd found and what they'd said. Then the time would be up, and the cuffs would go back on and Tim would take the slow walk back inside. He had crossed over, and he didn't know when, or even if, he would ever cross back.


Tim gave Patricia and Bill a four-page contact list of almost everyone he knew. Grace Villazon took the list and began making calls and knocking on doors. Pretty soon, Grace, Patricia and Bill were deep into the lives of Tim Anderson and Rick Parker.

Rick's body had been divested of its secrets by his autopsy, but his mad, bad life was far harder to unpick. It had three centres for a start: Florida, Houston and LA. He had two families, six or seven addresses, several cars and two drivers licences. He had a nickname and an alias. He told no one everything. His life was like a half-closed drawer full of knives. Grace dipped her hand in. She found Town and Country Transportation, the cab company which had taken Rick from the airport to the Embassy Suites in Lake Buena Vista. She contacted the EZ Pawn shop where Rick had stopped to pledge the boxing glove necklace and chain. The EZ Pawn computer confirmed that Rick had hocked the necklace in January too, and only got it out again seven days before his death. She went to the Embassy Suites to see if staff recognised the names on the contamination sheet that listed everyone who had entered and exited room 250. She spoke to Cheryl Hook at the Sand Lake Hospital. She located two former employees of Rick's, John Levesque and Ali Roberson. Levesque told her that Roberson showed up on 29 April in Fat Rick's car and carrying his California driver's licence and told him that Rick had been shot. Roberson left the car and took the licence. The car was repo-ed. Grace asked Levesque about Rick. He told her, 'Rick couldn't even sleep straight'.

Grace looked at what Rick had left in room 250. She saw his razor, his mouthwash and his toothbrush. She saw an interim driver's licence in his name issued to an address in Benedict Canyon Drive, Beverly Hills. She saw prescriptions for doxycycline and Benconase from a doctor in Temple, Texas. She saw a business card for 'Excellent Sales – John Levesque and Luis Rodriguez: Guadeloupe, Barcenas, 472 East Witcher'. She saw a traffic citation for a David Lee Bailey, who gave an address in San Mateo and a date of birth of 9/26/1968. She saw a copy of his civil action against *Sports Illustrated* magazine. She saw a receipt for jewellery worth $125 from a pawnshop in Jonesboro, Georgia. She saw a list of phone numbers dialled from a Sheraton hotel room. She saw an address for an 'R. Parker' in Springs, Texas. She saw the registration ticket from the Embassy Suites, issued to 'Jim Nelson' at an address in Memphis, Tennessee.

A half-closed drawer full of knives. From these fragments and fractions they had to assemble their case. Fat Rick had his three lives, his one death and his secrets. No one knew all of them, no one at all.

Within a month of meeting Patricia and Bill, Tim asked them if they thought he could beat the death rap. He no longer actively wanted it. Some days he didn't care. Others, he cared a lot. Others still were long slabs of grey in which he didn't even think about it. He was edging back into life. His health improved marginally . His body sometimes felt like it was his again. Bill told him that they would try everything they could. Diane McVay was their brightest hope. She was Rick's sister and next of kin, someone that the State would listen to in the penalty phase of the case, after verdict and before sentencing. They spent many hours with her. Patricia and Bill felt she would hold up. They needed to find out everything they could about the fight in Oklahoma City and about Tim's illness. They had to demonstrate exactly what took him to the Embassy Suites with a gun in his hand. Defences like Tim's built cumulatively. One piece of evidence allowed them to enter the next piece of evidence, the next added to its weight. They began to criss-cross the state in search of the people who could help them do it.

Sometimes when the cell doors were locked and the strip lights were off, when the chimes and clangs and squeaks of the prison night sang out, Rick appeared and stood before him. He was a figure of smoke, a time-ghost, a blurry but tangible avatar from his distant universe. He'd remove his sunglasses and talk. His voice still came through thin and high and clear; a tough guy's voice. A bad guy's voice.

Tim didn't find it strange to see him. Rick came because he represented all of the fear and doubt that Tim felt but could not reveal. Rick told Tim things, things about Ellis Rubin and why he'd disappeared from the case almost as soon as he'd arrived. Rick whispered to him about Diane – told him that she needed money, and someone might give her some to keep away from court. Rick said that he still had people on the outside, people who were making threats to Tim via the warders. Rick said that if he thought Erin was safe, then he'd better think again.

Tim didn't tell Bill and Patricia about it. He didn't want them to think he'd gone nuts. But there were things that had happened to him that didn't belong in court. Like the gun he'd taken to the Embassy Suites, the gun that had jammed and then unjammed and then jammed again. The gun that had killed Rick and spared his own life. The voice that had come into his head, telling him that it wasn't his time. How do you make sense of something like that? How do you tell a court?

'Death is still on the table,' that's what Bill said.

'Well, Bill,' Tim wanted to say, 'death is always on the table, wherever you are.'

You just couldn't tell. You could never really tell.

To Bill McClellan, boxing was wild and bizarre. How could a jury understand it? Everything Tim had told them was turning out to be true. Bill and Trish and Grace travelled for weeks, talking to people who they hoped could help. Don Hazelton opened the doors. He gave them the depositions he'd taken. He told them lots of great stories about Fat Rick that were hearsay and could never be admitted into court. They read through Tim's deposition to the Florida State Athletic Commission and his intake interview with Ellis Rubin and the notes they'd taken themselves. His story was rock-solid, unchanging.

They found David McMillan, a former partner of George Foreman's, and Steve Benson, who had handled publicity down in Fort Lauderdale. They found Rob Russen and Kevin Finn. They found Billy Cotter and Bill Lucci. They found Denis Jones and Jimmy Glenn. In the office one night, Patricia said to Bill, 'You know, this is a lot more cut-throat than I would ever have believed. Way more violent, way more corrupt. This is *sleazy* . . .'

They decided that Tim Anderson was the best asset they had. He was a good guy in a universe of bad guys. It shone through. It would be very hard for someone to say that Tim Anderson deserved to die once they'd seen the case from his point of view.

They had to get the story out there, and not just at the trial. They had the District Attorney's office leaking and briefing all kinds of crap. To the readers of newspapers and the watchers of news programmes, to the potential jurors at the trial of Tim Anderson, he was a washed-up, punch-drunk loser with an imagined grudge, just another seedy guy from a seedy world. He'd lured his victim to his death with a fairy story; he'd not just decided to kill him, he'd decided to torture him, starting by shooting him in his knees and working his way up the body, reloading as he went, making sure he planted the symbolic money shot – a bullet in the dick.

They hired a media relations specialist called Margaret Mackenzie to work on the case. It was the first time anything like it had happened in Florida – they were spending public dollars to spin a murder case. Margaret believed the death penalty to be morally wrong. She agreed to cut her usual fee.

She met Tim in the front room of the Orange County Jail. She shaped the parts of his story he would share with reporters. She asked for photographs of him and Erin together. She told him to forget about shaving his head. She told him not to accept collect calls from reporters. She told him not to allow prison personnel to add reporters to his visitors' list. She told him never to discuss his belief in God. She arranged for him to speak to Gerald Shields at the *Orlando Sentinel*, because Gerald Shields was a writer she could trust.

Bill and Patricia began filing motions. They had a good judge for the case, Judge Robert Evans. His appointment was a lucky break. They went to war on the DA's office. On 21 December 1995 they filed three motions against death.

On 24 January they filed four motions against death.

On 14 February they filed eight motions against death.

Death remained on the table.

Gerald Shields' story about Tim ran on the front page of the *Orlando Sentinel* one Sunday, with a double-page follow-up inside. There was a dramatic shot of Tim in jail on the front. Inside was a big picture of Tim and Erin. The headline was 'Ex-Boxer Faces The Fight Of His Life'.

Tim gave an interview to a Florida TV news channel that ran over two nights and covered everything from the poisoned water to the car-park beatings. Tim's voice, soft and mournful, told his story.

He might have been a killer. But he no longer looked like a murderer. Not Tim. Not this gentle man, grey with regret.

As they looked through State witness lists, sifted statements, chased down boxers, promoters, trainers, cornermen and crossroaders and kayfabe artists, Patricia and Bill felt the weight of the case against them. They could break it down into a simple sentence: two men walked into a room; one man walked out. There was no way around it, nothing beyond it. Tim Anderson had taken a gun to room 250 of the Embassy Suites. He had come up with a story to get Rick Parker there. He had left notes to his loved ones implying that something was about to happen. He had shot Rick Parker at least eleven times, reloading the gun twice. He had made a four-hour confession to police, stating that he had tortured and killed Fat Rick by shooting him from the ground up. He'd said he wanted the death penalty.

These things Trish and Bill could not set aside. Instead they tried to establish mitigation. They obtained Tim's

medical records and ordered toxicology tests to try and prove
the poisoning. They sought to establish Tim's attempts to
publish a book called *Liars, Cheats and Whores*. They
obtained an affidavit from Denis Jones that said Rick Parker
always carried a gun in his silver briefcase. They had Diane
write to the State Prosecutor asking that they not consider the
death penalty. They obtained the cooperation of Don
Hazelton and Jack McLaughlin. Don and Ron Russen opened
up on Rick's business dealings. Steve Benson and David
McMillan provided evidence of Parker's threats and
demeanour. Jim Murphy knew the history of Tim's last years
with Rick.

They obtained the FBI's records on the investigation into
Rick Parker under freedom of information laws. The files
arrived struck through with black lines. They asked the
Federal Government to turn over the information they had on
Rick Parker's activities. The Government refused.

They submitted a witness list that included Steve Benson,
Don Hazelton, Denis Jones, Rick MacAllister, Jack
McLaughlin, David McMillan, Diane McVay, Jim Murphy,
Rob Russen, Suzanne Migdall and Richard Smitten.

They tried to break down the State witness list, thirty
names that included George Anderson and Erin Anderson-
O'Brock. Their presence on the list meant that they would
not be permitted to sit in court.

Late in February 1996, a police officer failed to appear for a
hearing before Judge Robert Evans. Evans got pissed off,
remanded the officer into custody, had him handcuffed and
taken to jail. It caused quite a stir at the courthouse. The
Chief Judge removed Robert Evans from the criminal bench
and sent him to the civil division. He was no longer the judge
at the trial of Tim Anderson.

Judge Richard Conrad was allocated in his place. All of
the Public Defenders knew Conrad. Bill and Trish had

appeared before him many times. They knew he was short-tempered. They knew they'd have to fight him hard on issues that they could have slipped past Evans.

In the few moments that it took Robert Evans to lose patience with a tardy cop, Tim Anderson's chances diminished by a few more degrees.

Two weeks before the trial was due to begin and without any particular warning, the State took death off the table. A terse statement from the State Attorney's office read, 'The circumstances surrounding the case do not warrant the death penalty.'

Tim came up from the inside of the jail to the room at the front to hear the news. Bill and Trish looked at him, with his broken mind and his broken body and his broken heart. At least he wouldn't die at their hands. Tim smiled.

Bill and Trish revised their best-case scenarios. They'd enter a not-guilty plea citing self-defence. They felt they could get murder in the second, maybe an unlikely manslaughter.

They revised their worst-case scenarios too. Under Florida law, there was a mandatory sentence of life without parole for a conviction for murder in the first degree when the State did not seek death. Under Florida law, the jury were not told of this condition before reaching a verdict. Under Florida law, there was no plea of temporary insanity, only total insanity and incarceration in a mental institution. Under Florida law, any kind of diminished capacity could only be argued in the penalty phase of the case, as a mitigating factor in sentencing; and there would be no penalty phase in a case with a mandatory sentence. Under Florida law, Tim Anderson had nowhere to go; he had to take the high-risk strategy.

Houston Perkins came from Oklahoma City. Grace Villazon found him. At the end of February, on leap-year day, she'd been given the names of two men who might have refereed the fight between Tim Anderson and Mark Gastineau at the

Myriad Arena. One was Houston Perkins and the other was
Steve Thomasson. She located Houston Perkins. He told her:
'It was me.'

Bill, Trish and Grace deposed Houston by telephone from
Oklahoma City three days before they heard that death was
coming off the table. Dorothy Sedgwick represented the State.
All four sat together in Dorothy's office on North Orange
Avenue, with Houston on speaker phone. His voice blew in
from down the line, three parts human, one part tin. He was
thirty years old. As a kid he'd been a boxer, an amateur, but
he'd grown disillusioned and had become a referee instead.
He was just nineteen when he handled his first fight. Over
the next eleven years, Houston logged over twelve hundred
bouts in the little record book he kept. He'd met Fat Rick
through Sean Gibbons. Sean was a friend and partner of Pete
Susens. Houston had met Tim, too, he said, over at the TV
commentator Sean O'Grady's house. Sean O'Grady was Sean
Gibbons' cousin.

When Rick made the match between Mark and Tim at the
Myriad, Sean Gibbons called Houston and asked him to
referee.

Houston knew all about Fat Rick. He'd heard that when
you shook Rick Parker's hand, you counted your fingers
afterwards.

Tim had seemed fine when he climbed into the ring.
Houston looked right into his eyes to make sure. He even
smelled him, to make sure he wasn't drunk or high. He
checked that his gumshield was in and his protector was on
and his shoelaces were tied. Then the fight was delayed
because Tim didn't have a water bottle or a mouthpiece or
something, but they'd got by and the bell had finally rung.

'I remember Tim just telling me something about him
being dizzy and stuff like that, but he never came out and
said, "Someone did this to me", or anything like that,'
Houston said.

'Tim just mentioned, "Hey, I'm getting dizzy and light-headed and nauseous" and you know, a bunch of other symptoms he was telling me he was getting. Basically that was it. And then I put the two of them together, he might have been telling me, I don't know.'

'I stopped it on . . . I'm trying to remember right. I've been here lately trying to remember exactly what the call was anyway. Tim was complaining about him being dizzy and stuff and I can't remember if he quit during the round or if he just got knocked down and didn't get back up and said, "No, I can't do it any more". I can't remember exactly what happened.'

Houston said he had written down 'TKO' in his records when he'd got home. Then he'd forgotten all about it. Doc Chumley, the ringside physician, told him that Tim had been poisoned. And then, just last November, on his way home from a hunting trip, Doc Chumley had been killed in a plane accident.

Houston Perkins finished talking. They thanked him and hung up the phone.

One day, not yet and not at the trial, but one day, they would understand why Rick Parker had chosen Oklahoma City as the location for the fight. Oklahoma City, with its winter storms and its metal skies, its aliens and with its secrets, with its singing voices travelling down distant lines.

Bill McClellan felt a little like a prize fighter himself. He was all wired and ghosted, hyped on a combination of adrenalin, fear, tension and hope. He'd spent hundreds, perhaps thousands, of hours preparing for the Anderson trial. They'd had weeks on the road, on the freeways, under the sun, meeting hostile witnesses, seeing people who didn't want to see them. They'd untangled knots, they'd developed theories and arguments and mitigations. The State's case was formidable, the judge was stern. Yet he had belief, belief for

Timothy Anderson, belief in Timothy Anderson and the story he told them.

Judge Conrad worked on the number of witnesses. Rob Russen was told the day before the trial that he wouldn't be required. Denis Jones was at the airport ready to fly to Orlando, when he was paged and told that he was released from the subpoena. The size of the story Tim could tell grew smaller.

Bill would make the opening remarks for the defence. He knew how hard Dorothy Sedgwick would come in: the trap, the gun, the reloads, the confession. She had simplicity on her side.

He worked on a rebuttal that took her simplicity as its starting point and spun it around. He wanted to show the jury the forces that had delivered Tim Anderson to a hotel room with a gun in his hand. He wanted to show the jury who was the bad guy here. He wanted to establish the relationship between Rick Parker and Tim Anderson in their minds. He wanted to bring Fat Rick back from wherever he was; the size of him, his weight, his heft, his aura. He wanted to sketch Tim's state of mind, his love for his family, his fear for their lives. He wanted to take Dorothy Sedgwick's simple, cold worldview and undermine it. He worked it and worked it. He felt a little like he thought a fighter might feel, getting ready to fight a bigger man.

The trial of Tim Anderson began at 3.15 p.m. on 13 May 1996. Rick Parker had been dead for 382 days. Judge Conrad welcomed the jury, then he laid down the law, actual and implied. He sat at the head of the court in a black robe, his necktie visible above the zipper of the robe. He was a heavy-set man, but his features balanced it. He was saturnine, slightly grey, a man of the indoors, of the lower air. Tim Anderson sat at a table before him in a blue suit with a blue shirt and a coloured tie. His hair was cut and he was freshly shaved. His face was still taut on its fine bones, his neck tight with tension, but, underneath, something of the athlete remained in his unconscious movement, in his ease with his body. He was a creature of the upper air, a rare thing. Bill and Trish sat on either side of him. After a brief recess so that jurors could find the coffee machine and the jury room, Dorothy Sedgwick got to her feet, and it began.

When it was done, four days later, Bill McClellan still wasn't entirely sure when, or even if, things had gone wrong. It buzzed and roared through his mind; he played sections of it over and over. He was exhausted but too tired to sleep. He was hungry but too tense to eat. Some trials left him quickly, but this one was deep inside him, inside all of them. It would not be easily forgotten.

It had started well enough. Dorothy opened as they thought she would. She played up the two years before the shooting, when Fat Rick had left south Florida and no one had seen him. She sketched Tim as embittered and vengeful, cruel enough to lure a man from out of state and take his son along to see him die. She told the court that Tim had shot Rick Parker from the knees up, had shot him in the penis. She said she would play the jury his taped confession. She said that the state would not be bothering with the events of the distant past. Everything the jury needed to know happened in that hotel room.

When she'd finished, Bill stood up, felt his knees shake and said simply: 'Things aren't so complicated. Yes, Rick Parker is dead. Yes, Timothy Anderson shot him. The question here is why.'

He paused. Then he redrew Dorothy's opening. He ran her film backwards. Good became bad, bad became good. Here was Fat Rick redux, perpetually surrounded by his paid-for goons, gun in his boot, sizzling weave on his great red head, spewing his threats, spending his money, running his race. Here was Tim Anderson, exploited and duped, beaten and poisoned, with all of his deepest fears played upon, doing the only thing he could do: defend himself. Bill sat down. Tim swallowed and smiled.

The first State witnesses were the firefighters and the EMTs and the cops, the bellhops and the night managers and the receptionists from the Embassy Suites. Trish handled the cross-examinations. In the remainder of the afternoon, they got through Jerome Walker Jnr, Kevin Wiltz, Christopher Francisco and James Ward. The next morning, it was Mike Vasquez, Heather Mason, Phillip Bailey, Phillip Kennedy and Vicky Pettys. The firefighters and the cops were well acquainted with unexpected death. When they described it to the court, it sounded like just another day at work. The Embassy Suites staff had been unwilling to indulge Dorothy Sedgwick in lurid descriptions of the scene.

Day two had been the day, Bill thought afterwards, day two had been the day Rick Parker had spoken, the day that Fat Rick had his say. Day two had been the day of Detective John Linnert and Doctor Thomas Hegert, of Diane McVay and Chris Parker, the day the jury saw Rick naked and dead, they day that they heard Tim Anderson confess, the day that Bill McClellan and Trish Cashman could not turn their way.

Diane had come to the stand first. If Dorothy hadn't called her for the prosecution, Bill and Trish would have called her anyway. She had that same quick brain as Rick, that same verbal dexterity. She was smart and funny. When Dorothy asked her if she'd noticed any bulges in Tim's clothing as they drove to the Embassy Suites, Diane replied, 'I don't go around looking for bulges', and everyone except Dorothy

Sedgwick laughed. Diane described the days before the shooting. She described the events at the hotel. She told them how Rick was and how Tim was. She believed absolutely in what Rick had done to Tim. She agreed that she and Tim had once been lovers. She did not believe Tim had planned to kill Rick, and did not know he had a gun.

Chris Parker gave his account of the night at the Embassy Suites. He had ended it fatherless, with his shirt soaked in blood. His life had changed in the long year since; Rick's house had gone, one of the few constants he'd had. Fifteen years old, angry and lost, he left the stand and the courtroom. Then his face appeared at the glass in the door and he banged and shouted at Tim. They broke for lunch.

Dr Thomas Hegert showed them all diagrams of the gunshot wounds and the bullet paths he found at the autopsy. He showed them the bullets with his identifying marks on their casings. He explained patiently which wounds were fatal and which were not. Then he showed them the photographs of Rick in full colour on 35mm slides, with the court lights dimmed so they could study it in detail. Here was Rick's naked body, pictured in sections, with its red wound coins on the livid skin, with its peeling toupee, with the eyes half closed and the mouth slightly open, a small mark on the lip.

Doctor Hegert took everyone through the pictures, gunshot by gunshot. He told them that there was no way of knowing the order in which they had occurred. He left them with colour prints for examination in the jury room. Bill McClellan sighed.

Detective John Linnert gave his evidence next. It consisted almost entirely of Tim's taped confession. Tim's voice rose from the machine. It fought through the tape hiss, an insect whirr of buzzing wings, rubbing legs. It flared and bounced. Judge Conrad frowned and glowered. Bill and

Trish sat and listened. Tim zoned in and out. He already knew what he'd said.

There were five sides of tape. After two of them, Conrad sent the jury out for a fifteen-minute recess and called Dorothy and Trish to the bench.

'What's going on here?' he asked. 'There's no issue at all that he committed the murder – am I mistaken here? Am I missing something? No? Then why am I listening to this? Is this a trial about the history of boxing from 1988, or is this a trial about premeditated murder in the first degree?'

Dorothy explained that she'd wanted to redact the tapes, to play only parts to the jury. Trish hadn't. For Trish, the tapes offered Tim the chance to tell his back story, to get it before the jury in a way that the judge wouldn't let him do in open court. Trish argued hard. Tim would be hugely compromised if everything before the shooting was omitted. Conrad agreed. The jury returned to court and the tapes were played for the rest of the day.

Bill sat silently, not looking at Trish, not looking at Tim, listening to the voice through the insect chorus of the squawking tape and thinking, 'This is bad. This is very bad . . . I don't know if we can get him past this.'

Bill went back to his office, didn't eat, didn't sleep and pretty soon he was in court again. Before they opened the case for the defence, a Senior Crime Laboratory Analyst called Susan Komar came to explain one of the earthly mysteries of the Embassy Suites. She had carried out ballistics tests on Tim Anderson's gun.

'It was found that the revolver does malfunction,' she said. 'It can be fired but there are times when the cylinder seems to lock up or bind and the cylinder won't rotate. If the cylinder won't rotate, you can't do anything. There is something with the internal mechanism; either the hand in relation to the mechanism sticks or jams up or the cylinder release does not release properly sometimes.'

But why it fired eleven times into Rick Parker and then jammed in Tim Anderson's mouth, why it fired into the ground and then jammed in Tim Anderson's mouth again, why it killed Rick and spared Tim, Susan Komar could not explain.

When Bill and Trish opened the defence they couldn't get a damn thing right. They called David McMillan, George Foreman's associate. David said Rick Parker told him he was going to 'fuck Tim Anderson up', but then he admitted that he hadn't passed the threats on to Tim and Judge Conrad threw his evidence out.

They did better with Steve Benson. Steve said Rick Parker threatened him and his wife, said he'd kill his dogs and burn his house down. Fat Rick had shown Steve his gun. Steve said he'd lived in terror.

They did okay with Don Hazelton. He told them he'd turned Fat Rick over to Jack McLaughlin and the FBI. Jack McLaughlin confirmed it all.

They got Christina Nielson, Jim Murphy's former girl-friend, on the stand. She told them about the Tim Anderson she knew: the thin and suffering man who shared Jim's house, always falling down stairs and sleeping for days. They got Jim Murphy on the stand. He told them about the Tim Anderson he knew: the pitcher with the terrific slider; the glowing guy who fought George Foreman and Larry Holmes; the sunny, happy, teetotal athlete. Then he told them about the Tim Anderson that shuffled back from Oklahoma City.

'He was destroyed . . . The guy was almost a vegetable.'

They got Houston Perkins on the stand. Houston Perkins, their chattering alien from the naked-eye universe, who said that he refereed the fight in Oklahoma City but who couldn't remember how it had ended.

They tried to get a toxicologist called Bruce Goldberger on the stand to say that Tim was most likely poisoned with LSD, but Conrad said it was too speculative and threw it out.

They tried to get Richard Smitten on the stand to say that he and Ellis and Tim were talking about writing a book, and they tried to get Suzanne Migdall on the stand to say that Tim had asked for help to put his book together and had faxed her an outline of it. They wanted to prove that the book wasn't an invention, just an excuse to get Rick back to Orlando. Conrad said that there wasn't a signed book deal, just talk. He threw them both out.

Bill and Trish were done. Every witness who had something relevant to say, they had used, or tried to. They'd fought with Dorothy and with Conrad. They'd fought the confession and the book and the reloaded gun. There was only one person left to speak and that was Tim. It was late afternoon and too late for him to start so Conrad sent everyone home.

Bill went to his office, couldn't eat, couldn't sleep. He visualised himself asking the opening questions the next day. Soon enough, it began.

STATE OF FLORIDA, PLAINTIFF
VS
TIMOTHY ALLEN ANDERSON, DEFENDANT

CASE NO: CR95-5207

VOLUME IV TRIAL PROCEEDINGS
BEFORE THE HONOURABLE RICHARD CONRAD

P428

DIRECT EXAMINATION BY MR MCCLELLAN:

> Q: Tim, did you shoot Rick Parker on the night of
> April 28, 1995?
>
> A: Yes.
>
> Q: Did you at any time make a conscious decision
> to kill Mr Parker?
>
> A: No.
>
> Q: Were you in fear of your life in the hotel room?
>
> A: At that moment, I wasn't exactly in fear at
> that time.
>
> Q: Were you in fear for your sister's life?
>
> A: Yes.
>
> Q: Could you tell the jury why you went up to the
> hotel room last April?
>
> A: I had been drugged and poisoned in a fight in
> 1992, December. And I had found out in January
> that there was a poison in my system and that I
> talked to a toxicologist who . . .

And so it went on. Bill led him through it, good and loyal Bill. Tim talked and talked. He told his story in his slow, considered voice. He tried to answer the question that Bill had asked in his opening statement, the only question that he could possibly answer: Why. Why? But there were so many answers, so many reasons.

After an hour, it was Dorothy Sedgwick's turn. She ripped and tore at him. Bill and Trish couldn't keep her off him, but he didn't really mind. Why had he never told the police about Rick Parker's threats? Why had he bought a gun? Why had he lied about his book? Why had he written farewell letters to his family? Why had he shot Rick Parker so many times? Why had he said what he said to John Linnert? Why had he lied? Why? Why? Over and over, like a ticking clock, like hypnosis, like a dream. Why? Why? So many answers. So many reasons.

Just before the jury entered court for the final day, Judge Conrad did something remarkable. He allowed the sheriff to remove Tim's leg irons, so that he could walk unassisted to the stand.

'You've been good,' Conrad said. 'Don't let me down.'

Bill couldn't remember Conrad doing anything like it before. What did it mean? The clock moved sideways. It was a time for portents, a time for signals and signs. They had no real idea how they'd done, how the case had played for the jury, so they sat and they waited. Trish had closed hard. She blew through the State's case witness by witness. She added doubt where the State had claimed certainty. After she'd finished, Bill thought they had a shot at a lesser included, a murder in the second degree, perhaps a manslaughter. They had a shot, but that was all.

Tim was still deep on the inside. He was numb and grey. Was he guilty? He didn't think he knew any more. He decided to let them tell him. He sat in the holding cell waiting for the jury to come back. Trish asked him if he'd liked to address the court when the verdict came in. He told her that he would.

The jury returned just before ten o'clock on a Friday night. They had been sequestered for almost seven hours. They had elected a foreman, Vincent Runfola. They had requested a copy of the transcript of Tim's confession. They had considered the three choices that Judge Conrad had explained to them:

Premeditated murder in the first degree: That Richard Parker was dead; that the criminal act or agency of Timothy Allen Anderson had killed him; that the decision to kill was present in his mind at the time of the killing; that there was a period of reflection after the decision to kill and before the killing itself.

*[A man walks into a hotel room with a gun. He shoots the guy inside and walks out again. He gives the gun to the cops and spends two hours telling them exactly how he did it.]*

Murder in the second degree: That Richard Parker was dead; that the criminal act or agency of Timothy Allen Anderson had killed him; that there was an unlawful killing of Richard Parker by act imminently dangerous to another and evincing a depraved mind regardless of human life.

*[A man arranges to meet a former business partner at a hotel because he needs some information. He tries to shake the guy up by pointing a gun at him. His mind goes blank and, the next thing he knows, his former business partner is lying dead at his feet.]*

Manslaughter: That Richard Parker was dead; that Timothy Allen Anderson intentionally caused the death of Richard Parker, or that the death of Richard Parker was caused by the culpable negligence of Timothy Allen Anderson.

*[A man meets a former business associate at a busy hotel. They argue. One panics and shoots the other and then attempts to shoot himself.]*

Vincent Runfola handed a slip of paper to the clerk.

Richard Conrad said: 'Madam clerk, would you publish the verdict please?'

The clerk said: 'Indictment CR95-5207, State of Florida versus Timothy Allen Anderson. We the jury find the defendant guilty of murder in the first degree in the indictment, so say we all, the sixteenth day of May, 1996.'

Bill turned white and fell back in his chair. He thought he might puke. He turned and looked at Tim Anderson. Tim's expression hadn't changed, but his jaw was bunched and the vein in his temple ticked like a bomb.

Trish Cashman asked that the jury be present for sentencing. Chris Parker gave his victim impact statement. He said he'd be waiting for Tim Anderson if he ever got out. Conrad nodded at Trish.

Trish said: 'Your honour, the law of the State of Florida is such that the court has no discretion, it is your duty to sentence Mr Anderson to life in prison with no possibility of parole. Tim wishes to be heard.'

The court was utterly quiet. The jurors stared at Tim. His leg irons made a gentle swish as he stood.

'I just want to say I'm very sorry to everyone in my family and to everyone here today.' He sat down again. Trish put her hand on his arm.

Conrad handed down the sentence and thanked the jury. He told them that they were free to discuss the case with the media if they wished. He gave Tim Anderson thirty days to appeal. It was exactly 10 p.m.

Outside the courtroom, there was chaos. George and Erin were surrounded. They had glimpsed Tim briefly after the sentencing. The subpoena had kept them out of court, on the outside. The jury hadn't seen them, hadn't heard them.

The day after the trial, the jury foreman Vincent Runfola wrote to Judge Conrad. His letter read: 'We were all going to write you a letter during the pre-sentence investigation, requesting leniency for Mr Anderson. We now know that we never had that chance. Most of the jury members walked out of the courtroom feeling blindsided.'

A jury member, Felicia Waters, also wrote to Conrad and sent the letter to a newspaper. It read: 'Once we agreed the verdict, many of us cried and silence filled the room for what seemed like an eternity. It was then that we all decided to write you a letter prior to Mr Anderson's sentencing to request leniency. At the time, we had no idea that on returning to the courtroom that Mr Anderson would be sentenced to life in prison with no chance of parole. Most of us left that evening feeling shocked and misled.'

Something from Dorothy Sedgwick's closing argument hung in the air, something that stayed with many people. 'We're in a court of law, and a court of law has its limitations,' she'd said. 'A court of law cannot correct all the wrong things done in the world, it can't turn back time. It can't.'

All the wrong things done in the world. Wasn't that a line.

The trial of Tim Anderson had been a simple one. It came down to this: two men walked into a room. One man walked out.

All of it was true. None of it was true.

Tim was taken down to the inside, underneath the razor wire, behind the wall, under the sun. Bill and Patricia didn't see him again for many years.

# Noir Boxers

*[Deep on the inside, locked away and alone, Tim Anderson remains connected . . . connections are how things work here . . . how things work in the naked-eye universe . . . in the naked-eye universe of boxing . . . Follow their trails . . . link their chains . . . visit their places . . . Tim to Rick . . . Rick to Mark . . . Mark to Oklahoma City . . . Oklahoma City to Houston Perkins . . . Houston Perkins to Steve Thomasson . . . Steve Thomasson to Sean Gibbons . . . Sean Gibbons to Pete Susens . . . Sean and Pete to Bob Arum . . . Bob Arum to Don King . . . Don King to Bert Cooper . . . $50 Bert to Fat Rick . . . Fat Rick to Doc Anderson . . . Inside to outside . . . outside to in . . . Follow their trails . . . Link their chains . . . Feel their breath . . . Feel their breath . . .]*

18 June 1979. A boy named Joey Torres shot and killed another boy named Armando Cardenas Jasso in the back office of a Texaco gas station on Florence Avenue in Downey, California. Joey was nineteen years old and Armando was twenty-three. Joey's real name was Kim

Joseph Torres, but the people around Downey called him 'Boxer'. He'd won an AAU title for amateur fighters in 1976.

It took the cops a few days to figure out what happened. Joey took off for New Orleans, but he came back a fortnight later and they arrested him. Joey began to tell his story. He was in the office of the gas station for a meeting with Jasso, who was his boxing manager. They argued. Jasso pulled a gun. Joey wrestled it from him and used it in self-defence.

'Joey,' the detective told him, 'this looks bad for you. The kid's dead. We got you holding the gun. The safe is open. The money's gone. You took off for New Orleans. We gotta work something out.'

So they worked something out. Joey Torres pled guilty to murder. He would serve time with the California Youth Authority until he was twenty-five. If he stayed out of trouble he'd be free. If he didn't, it was twenty-five to life. Joey didn't. He was accused of trying to get a girlfriend to smuggle a gun into the facility. He was transferred to State prison, where he stayed for more than twenty years.

On 1 March 1993, Tex Cobb knocked out Mike Smith in Kansas, Missouri. Mike Smith's record dropped to 3-10-1 and he incurred a mandatory thirty-day suspension.

Two weeks later, Mike Smith went to Jefferson City, Missouri, where he fought Art 'King Arthur' Jimmerson. He used the alias Shane Mooney to get around the suspension. And Shane Mooney was a dead man. He'd been dead for five months. Car crash. He was a white welterweight and Mike Smith was a black heavyweight, but no one seemed to notice. Art Jimmerson knocked out the dead man in round number two. On the same bill, a fighter called Marty Jakubowski boxed Craig Houk. Craig Houk used the alias Tim Bennett. And Tim Bennett was another dead man.

Two years later, at a boxing convention, the ratings chairman of the NABF, Claude Jackson, mentioned Tim Bennett to Jacob Hall, the boxing commissioner of Indiana. Jacob felt that Claude's description of Bennett sounded a lot like Craig Houk. When he returned to his office, he pulled Bennett's licence application and drove to the home address written on the form. It was a cemetery.

Around that time, a man named Jose Venzor got the idea that he could make himself a lot of money promoting a title defence by a Mexican boxer called Julio Cesar Chavez in Chicago. Julio Cesar Chavez was a Don King fighter. He'd been to the ring on ninety-seven occasions and won ninety-five times. He was Mexico's raging bull, an indomitable boxer, an embodiment of his people's pride and spirit. Julio was getting old. He was hanging on for a superfight with a new Hispanic hero, Oscar de la Hoya, a fight that would make both of them millions of dollars. While he waited, he wanted some quieter paydays. He'd earned them.

Jose Venzor wanted Chavez in Chicago. Don King Productions contracted to provide Jose with Julio and a worthwhile opponent for a night of boxing. The opponent they came up with was Craig Houk. They sold him to Jose Venzor as a tough guy with forty-seven wins and six defeats on his record, a tough guy who would give the great Chavez a good night's work.

Jose thought Craig Houk sounded perfect. He hired the Rosemont Horizon. He agreed to pay Craig Houk $50,000 and Julio Cesar Chavez a whole lot more. Julio knocked Craig Houk out in seventy-nine seconds. The Rosemont Horizon was almost empty. Jose discovered that there weren't many Mexican fight fans in Chicago.

Jose Venzor had collided with the naked-eye universe. It cost him a lot of money. He realised that in boxing you could only trust what you saw for yourself. And he saw Craig Houk getting knocked out before the fucking bell had stopped ringing. He hired an attorney called Bob Orman and sued Don King Productions, alleging breach of contract, fraud, consumer fraud, deceptive business practices, violating Illinois boxing regulations and violating the federal civil racketeering statutes.

It didn't take Bob Orman's investigators long to find out who Craig Houk was. He was Tim Bennett and he was also Gary Meyers. Tim Bennett was a far worse boxer than Craig Houk. His record was 5 and 19. And Gary Meyers was a far worse boxer than Tim Bennett. His record was 0 and 7. Tim Bennett and Gary Meyers both had false social security numbers and different dates of birth.

Craig Houk's official record of 47 and 6 did not mean 47 and 6. He had fought Marty Jakubowski five times, Tim Brooks four times, Kenny Willis twice, Julio Ibarra twice, Kenneth Kidd twice, David Pearson twice and Rocky Berg twice.

Tim Bennett's record of 5 and 19 didn't mean 5 and 19 either. He'd fought Rocky Berg four times and Terry Thomas twice.

Craig Houk had beaten Rocky Berg twice, but Tim Bennett had lost to him four times. Rocky Berg had an alias, too. Under the name Rocky Vires, he fought Craig Houk twice more. Houk won both times.

Jose Venzor's lawsuit stated that he never would have accepted Craig Houk as an opponent for Julio Cesar Chavez had he been aware of his record or his aliases. He alleged that Don King Productions knowingly misrepresented Houk's record and his skills as a fighter. He alleged that Houk was telephoned by Don King Productions and told to use his talent and ability to make sure he lost to Julio Cesar Chavez. Don King Productions denied everything.

The lawsuit tumbled into dark space. It was settled out of court. It meant nothing to Don King. Lawsuits were the language of boxing.

'He lost money,' Don said, 'and I'm at the top of the pole.'

After Jacob Hall had driven to Tim Bennett's home address and found himself in a cemetery, he began to check the licence applications of other fighters. A number appeared to have been filled out in the same handwriting. They all featured the same address, in Oklahoma City. It was that of Pat O'Grady. Pat was the father of Sean O'Grady, the *Tuesday Night Fights* ringside analyst, and the uncle of Sean Gibbons.

Everyone was connected. Sean Gibbons' best friend and long-time associate was the matchmaker Pete Susens. Jose Venzor's lawsuit alleged that Sean, Pete and a matchmaker called Fred Berns made up the 'Indiana–Oklahoma Connection'.

The Indiana–Oklahoma Connection provided twenty-five boxers to Don King Productions, only one of whom had won. Since 1989, they had criss-crossed the country in Sean Gibbons' car, which they filled up with fighters that they called the Knucklehead Boxing Club. They fought each other constantly for a couple of hundred bucks a time in clubs and bars, using false names and faked identities. They sat in Sean's white Honda as he put 300,000 miles on the clock, driving through the night to all those fights, pulling over to sleep at the sides of silent highways.

The Oklahoma Department of Labor began an investigation into boxing in Oklahoma and Indiana. The investigation was headed by W.A. 'Skip' Nicholson. It took two years. Skip called his report 'Allegations of Fraud and other Corruption in Boxing'. He presented it to the Oklahoma Department of Labor Commissioner Brenda Reneau in February 1997. Skip looked into the same universe as Jose Venzor and Bob Orman and he saw many of the same things.

A boxer named Verdell Smith testified that Sean Gibbons enabled him to get social security numbers for two aliases, Tim Bowles and Tim Brooks. A fighter called Keith Whitaker testified that Pete Susens 'took from the top and the bottom' of a fighter's purse: he failed to disclose the true fee to the boxer and then took a manager's cut from the remainder.

Further testimony indicated that Sean Gibbons and Pete Susens smuggled fighters across the border from Mexico, gave them fake IDs and paid them as little as $100 per fight. That they placed fighters in physical danger by having them compete outside their weight class and by providing fake documentation that allowed them to bypass medical suspensions. That they harboured fugitives and provided false documentation to fighters who were on the run from the law.

Skip Nicholson made copies of the report available to the FBI, the Internal Revenue Service, the Social Security Administration and to Senator John McCain, who had sponsored a Federal Boxing Bill designed to deal with fraud and corruption in professional boxing.

Joey Torres was many years into his sentence for the murder of Armando Jasso when he started working the prison phones. Up to ten hours a day he'd stand with the receiver under his chin, punching out numbers and calling up names. He no longer looked like the nineteen-year-old kid who began his time with the California Youth Authority. He was soft and pudgy. Prison tattoos were scrawled upon his body. No one called him Boxer any more.

He was using the prison phone to place collect calls to some of the biggest names in American sport. When he got lucky and he got through, he told them his story, the story of Boxer the boxer, who killed his manager in self-defence and had his career and his life snatched away. He told them that he'd started an organisation called Boxers Against Drugs and he needed their help. He persuaded them to attend collector card conventions and autograph shows to raise money.

Joey got through to baseball star Paul Molitor in a Chicago hotel room. They got so close that Paul used to say that Joey helped to talk him through a hitting slump.

Joey got through to the former world lightweight champion Carlos Palomino at his home in Topanga Canyon.

'How d'you get this number?' Palomino asked.

'I got my ways,' said Joey.

Joey called sports writers and newspaper offices, television companies and radio stations. He called Bob Arum and Don King. He created his own history. He told the story of himself so often he came to believe it. He shaped it so expertly that when he changed the name of Armando Cardenas Jasso to Jose Luis Ramirez, nobody bothered to check if it was true.

He'd served twenty-three years when his lawyers found a legal technicality on which he could appeal his sentence. Joey got bail. Paul Molitor put up $100,000 and bought him a car. Another baseball player called Eric Davis gave him a place to stay and some new clothes. Bob Arum let him hang out at the Top Rank offices in Las Vegas. Bruce Trampler, Bob's matchmaker, wrote a screenplay about his life. Fighter turned movie producer Ray 'Boom Boom' Mancini wanted to make it into a film.

All that the movie needed was a happy ending; Bob Arum and Bruce Trampler tried to give it one. They PRed Joey into a televised fight at the Anaheim Pond in California. Joey went on news programmes to tell his story of redemption. They loved Joey and called him the Ultimate Comeback Kid. Bruce Trampler found the worst light heavyweight he could to fight him, a guy called Perry Williams, who had been knocked out in round number one of his only professional bout.

Perry Williams knocked Joey on his ass with the first right hand of the fight. Joey got up and Perry Williams got so scared that he might win he didn't throw another punch. Joey knocked him down with a suspect left and scored a kayo in the second round. The crowd rioted in protest and sixteen people were arrested. Joey and Perry were both suspended by the State Commission for lack of ability.

Sometimes even a man like Bob Arum could get lost in the naked-eye universe. When Joey began showing up at Top Rank with a guy called Big Frankie and introduced him as his cousin, Bob gave them both a job scouting fighters.

Big Frankie was a hoot, a rough wise guy from back east with a million funny stories. He handed round business cards that said 'Big Frankie, YGJ & Co'. Frankie was soon firm friends with Bruce Trampler's right-hand man at Top Rank. His name was Sean Gibbons.

Big Frankie began working corners for Sean. Sean taught him how to look into the naked-eye universe. In return, Big Frankie told him about his wise-guy life, fencing everything from whisky to jewellery for the New Jersey mob. He talked a lot and he made it sound real good. There was only one thing that Big Frankie didn't tell Sean Gibbons: that his real name was Frank Manzione, and he was an officer with the New York Police Department, working undercover on secondment for the FBI.

On 6 January 2004, after a twenty-month investigation, the FBI raided the offices of Bob Arum's Top Rank in Las Vegas. They seized computers, boxing contracts, medical records, videotapes and the traps from the sinks in the bathrooms. Bob issued a statement saying that Top Rank would cooperate fully with the investigation. Seven days later, he fired Sean Gibbons for 'unspecified reasons'.

In his only public comments on the investigation, Frank Manzione said that he witnessed Sean Gibbons using drugs. He saw him complete a fraudulent medical form for a fighter who used a variety of aliases, and Gibbons told him that he was paying a doctor $300 to issue a medical certificate without an examination of the fighter.

Other details emerged. A heavyweight named Mitchell Rose claimed that Top Rank officials offered him $5,000 to take a dive against Eric 'Butterbean' Esch. He refused and knocked Butterbean out in two rounds.

Sean Gibbons matched a heavyweight named Brad Rone with Billy Zumbrun for a bout in Cedar City, Utah. It was a last-minute thing. Brad needed the $800 purse to fly to his mother's funeral in Cincinnati. Brad was no boxer: he'd lost twenty-six fights in a row. He was 80 pounds overweight. He had been refused a licence in Nevada because he was suffering from hypertension. He passed a cursory medical examination before the fight and then died of a heart attack in the ring, walking back to his corner at the end of the first round. He'd been so flustered on the journey to Utah he'd forgotten his boxing socks. He was thirty-four years old.

Joey Torres went back to jail. The deal he had made with the FBI to get Frank Manzione inside Top Rank hadn't been enough to save him. He went back to jail because he believed his own stories and he wouldn't stop telling them.

His lawyers offered Los Angeles prosecutors a plea bargain. Ordinarily, the prosecutors would have nodded it through: Joey had served most of his sentence and had helped the FBI out. But Deputy District Attorney Pamela Frohreich liked the stories Joey kept telling. He didn't sound rehabilitated to her. She talked to the detectives who had arrested him after the shooting in 1979. She went back through their twelve-page report line by line. It made no mention of Armando Jasso being Joey's boxing manager. He was a minimum-wage gas-station attendant who didn't own a gun. Joey's story of wrestling a weapon away from him and using it in self-defence didn't stand up when set next to the

$335 missing from the safe. And Joey had changed the name of Armando Jasso to Jose Ramirez in his stories.

Joey's parents gave a statement to the prosecutor. It said: 'He is a skilful fabricator of stories who can weave fact and fiction together in a most convincing manner.' Pamela Frohreich convinced a court that Joey should return to jail. She didn't convince Joey though. He took off for Mexico. He was on the run for almost three months before he was finally apprehended.

They knew better than to give Joey access to a telephone in the first place they sent him to, so he wrote a letter to his sister instead. It ended up with the Associated Press. It told a universal story in a universal voice. It was about Joey's fight with Perry Williams in California. It was all a fake, said Joey. It was all a fix.

Sean Gibbons had taken his medical for him, otherwise they would have found out that Joey had hepatitis C and was partially sighted.

Then Perry had come to Joey's hotel room for the pre-fight meeting, at which sickly grins and bad jokes were exchanged, at which the furniture was pushed aside, at which the fighters were shown how to make their fake punches look good by Sean Gibbons.

Joey's letter sounded like the truth. But then Joey was a liar. You really couldn't believe anything he said.

It was all a fake. It was all a fix. It was all a joke.

The FBI investigation into Top Rank folded in 2005 without anyone being charged. The case was closed after problems with an informant. Sean Gibbons was the only Top Rank employee who lost his job, and he soon found another one, working as a matchmaker for the Syucan organisation.

No charges came from the Oklahoma Department of Labor report into boxing either. It was quietly filed away, opened

only by sports writers for their periodic stories on boxing's
underbelly.

Sean Gibbons and Pete Susens denied everything. So did
Bob Arum and Bruce Trampler and Don King and everybody
else. Through the naked-eye universe it was easy to connect
them together, but, even once you had, its other law applied:
You could only believe what you saw for yourself.

After the FBI investigation was over, someone asked Big
Frankie about the company that he'd listed on the business
cards he gave out at Top Rank.

'YGJ & Co.,' he smiled. 'You're Going to Jail . . .'

Except no one went. No one went to jail except for Joey
Torres. And he was the one who'd called the Feds in the first
place.

On a clear June night in 1992, Sean Gibbons met Houston
Perkins in Omaha, Nebraska. They collected a carful of
fighters in Kansas City and drove to Bismarck, North Dakota.
It was a Sunday, two days after Tim Anderson had beaten
Mark Gastineau for the first time in San Francisco.

Houston hadn't gone to Bismarck to referee, he had gone
there to box. He fought Harold Miller at the bottom of a six-
bout bill and got knocked out in round number one. It was his
second professional contest.

Sean had travelled for a day to get there. He'd been
watching Tim fight Mark at the Civic Centre Auditorium.
He'd been watching Fat Rick rage at Tim Anderson.

'I got the hell out of San Francisco,' he said to Houston.

'I can't believe Tim whooped him,' Houston replied.

'Well, he's in trouble. We're going to get a rematch with
him. We're going to beat the heck out of him. Rick's mad as
hell at him. Tim cost him a lot of money.'

Six months later, when summer had gone and winter had
come, when snow and storms and darkness covered Oklahoma

City, when four people died on the frozen freeways, Sean
Gibbons helped Rick Parker to put on Anderson–Gastineau
II. He made some matches. He arranged the referee. And then
he left the arena before the fights started, along with Pete
Susens. Tim Anderson watched them go and thought right
then he might be in trouble.

Somehow, Houston Perkins had turned up at the trial of Tim
Anderson like a regular Martin Guerre. His evidence was
clear. Although he had met Sean Gibbons two days after the
San Francisco fight and was told that Tim refused to take a
dive, although he remembered Sean telling him 'Tim's in
trouble, Rick's mad as hell', although Houston 'was watching
for a dive or something like that', he didn't find it odd that the
fight ended, he said, with Tim unable to continue because he
was sick. Neither did the investigators or the lawyers or the
court. Houston slipped unnoticed into the witness box and
slipped out again, leaving behind only the mystery of why he
had come.

After Steve Thomasson watched Steve Canton's tape of
Anderson–Gastineau II, he was, he told Steve, blown away
by the whole thing. He remembered now what had happened.
    Sean Gibbons had called and asked him to do the job.
Thomasson said sure. The boxers came to town a few days
before the fight. They went on a radio show called *The Sports
Animal*. Doc Anderson and Tex Cobb had great fun with the
DJ. Doc was telling everyone what he was going to do to Mark
Gastineau. Steve watched him closely. He saw how fit he was.
    Rick Parker had been cool with him, hadn't stepped out of
line. He was always slapping Steve on the back and making
a joke. Sean had even asked him to fetch Rick from his hotel
room one day when he was late for a press conference. That
was when Steve found him playing his piano and singing so
loudly he hadn't heard his phone.

The crowd had been a disappointment. Only a couple of hundred people. Must have been the weather. Steve had given the fighters his instructions in the dressing room. The fight began normally. Tim was outboxing Mark. Steve's friend Bill Hoffman was the guy who shouted out, 'Hey, Steve, I got you ahead' between the rounds.

Tim got clocked and Steve went into his usual routine, waving the fight off and removing Tim's gumshield. Afterwards, he checked with Doc Chumley that Tim was okay, then he collected his money and went home.

The next time he'd heard of Tim Anderson was when Sean Gibbons told him he'd shot and killed Rick Parker.

Steve knew Houston Perkins. They'd refereed a lot of cards together at one time. He hadn't seen him for ten years. He had no idea why Houston had gone to Florida to testify that he had refereed the fight. It was just another thing that blew him away.

Steve and Mary Lynn Canton were blown away, too. Houston Perkins remembered that he refereed the fight, but he hadn't. Steve Thomasson forgot that he refereed the fight, but he had. It was the naked-eye universe again. You could only believe what you saw for yourself. And they saw Steve Thomasson refereeing the fight on Rick Parker's videotape.

Ken Rodriguez had brushed up against Sean Gibbons in his investigations for the *Miami Herald*. Andre Smiley told him that Sean had offered him bonuses to throw fights. Mike Smith said the same thing. Ken had asked Sean, and Sean told him that it was all a lie.

Ken retreated from the noir movie he found himself watching. He moved away from boxing, became part of a *Miami Herald* investigative team that won a Pulitzer. But he still thought of Fat Rick and Tim Anderson from time to time. He thought of Eric Esch and Tony Fulilangi, and he thought of Sonny

Barch, his crossroader, his gatekeeper. But pretty soon they were all just names in files in boxes in newspaper libraries, names and faces that ran together as time blurred them. These alien ghosts retreated into the reaches of their joke universe, their stories half-told and only half-remembered.

# Tim and Rick

## 2008

To reach the town of Bowling Green from Orlando, take I-4 out through Kissimmee to US Highway 27. At Lake Wales take State Road 60 to Bartow and then at Bartow take Highway 17 through Pembroke and Fort Mead to Bowling Green. Stay on the highway through the still, dusty town and then where the road dips and rises and heads for Wauchula and Arcadia, take a right onto State Road 62 by the Holiday Inn. Head west past the orange groves and the farmhouse driveways and scrubby pastures for a dozen miles or so and you will see a high white water tower rising above the flat land to the left. As you draw closer, there before you are the low-rise buildings that surround the tower, also white, also fenced, and guarded by sets of white sentry posts. Turn left on to the impeccably kept driveway and pass the neat flower beds and you will arrive at the Hardee Correctional Institution. It is here that Tim Anderson lives now.

He is fifty years old and his days are usually quiet ones. After the operations on his neck and throat, he has been restored to full health. He works out hard every morning to a set routine. He drinks a gallon of water a day and alternates a vegan and vegetarian diet in annual cycles. His hands are still fast and he has a six-pack you could lose a coin in – he's a lean and hard cruiserweight these days. Someone once told him that, the food aside, prison is the best place to train as a boxer – maybe that's true.

The horror of the shooting, and of his last years as a free man, have dulled with time. He and his family have made their reconciliations to its brutal truths. In the days that followed the trial, the jury members' letters to Judge Conrad made a few lines in the papers. Patricia Cashman and Bill McClellan offered Tim the chance to appeal, citing ineffective counsel, but he declined. Deadlines for further action on different and various grounds of appeal began to expire. For a long time, little happened.

After Steve Canton met the old man at his gym in Fort Myers and obtained Rick Parker's videotape of the fight in Oklahoma, he and Mary Lynn sought answers to the questions that Tim's trial left behind. All that they found were its strange ambiguities. Houston Perkins had perjured himself, but his account of the fight wasn't particularly different from the one that Steve Thomasson would give later. The nature of Tim's poisoning has never been medically established. Oklahoma City withholds its answers and retains its mysteries. Rick Parker's life still has its secrets.

Trish Cashman and Bill McClellan visited Hardee in the summer of 2007. It was the first time that they had seen Tim since the trial, but they had never forgotten his case. They hope that there may be some legal remedy against the length of his sentence, whether via the discovery of new evidence or the long-shot last resort of a clemency appeal.

The value of new evidence – the Oklahoma fight tape for example, and the perjury of Houston Perkins – is hard to assess. Tim's defence was one that built cumulatively: one plank of evidence admitted the next by demonstrating its relevance. How much these new facts affect the existing ones is almost impossible to know.

Other aspects of the case remain a source of wonder and mystery to Tim. He'd tried to shoot himself in the head, twice, with the gun that had just killed Rick. He was sure that he'd heard a voice telling him that it 'wasn't his time'. He finds it impossible to articulate how that made him feel. Then there was the old man who visited Steve Canton's gym on that February night. He had led to the discovery of the videotape of the fight with Mark, the tape that wasn't supposed to exist. Tim was always sure that he'd seen it that morning after the fight, playing on the TV in the corner of Rick's hotel suite and he turned out to be right. That makes him think about things he saw at the Embassy Suites, too. The gun in Rick's ankle holster that was never found. The pages from Rick's book that he'd read aloud. He is as sure of those things as he was of the tape.

The real reasons that he feared Rick Parker had stayed out of court. They stayed out because the people who knew about them were hostile witnesses from a hostile universe. They stayed out because Richard Conrad didn't find them relevant, because they didn't fit within the rigid paradigms of the law. No one in court heard about the near-deaths and deaths that really haunted Tim: the kid from the cleaning crew. Joe Derrick.

All of that stayed out.

Rick Parker had another life, too, one in which he wasn't Elvis or Fat Rick. To Chris Parker, and to his other children, he was a father. To Diane, and to his other two sisters, he was a brother, and to their children he was an uncle. Their feelings for him, and for his fate, were governed by factors beyond his time in boxing. Diane, though, had known him better than anyone, and, despite some obvious emotional conflicts, she retained a clear view of her brother. As she said at the trial: 'It was no surprise that someone killed Rick. The only surprise was it was Tim that did it.'

Perhaps strangely, Tim never dreams of Rick. Whatever part of his subconscious Rick inhabits, it lies close to the place that holds his buried memories of the shooting. But Tim thinks of him still, and not always of the bad times. Occasionally, usually when he's not expecting it, there he is, Fat Rick Parker, back with him in all of his force, so close that he can almost feel him. Black slacks and red sports coat. A floral shirt and cowboy boots. The great red hairpiece on his head. A small smile across his face, still talking, still talking.

# Epilogue

George Foreman retired from boxing in 1997 after a comeback that had generated many millions of dollars and turned him from a dark and forbidding presence into one of the most avuncular figures in American life. He went on to make even more money selling his famous George Foreman Grills. Rick Parker's vision for him had proven acute.

Smokin' Bert Cooper fought on until 2002. He lost seven of his last ten fights before slipping back into the life that he had come from. There was no glorious second act for Bert, although fight fans still talk of that magic right hand.

Tex Cobb continues to appear in films and television shows, mostly as an extremely hairy, expressionless tough guy. He remarried and moved to Philadelphia, where he, too, is remembered by fight fans as a warrior.

After her divorce from Tex, Sharon Cobb endured some of the most difficult times of her life. She moved back to Nashville and now writes a popular and respected blog on American politics.

Mark Gastineau fought four times after Oklahoma. His

final bout came in 1996 in Japan, against another former NFL player, Alonzo Highsmith. Alonzo TKOed Mark in round number two. He served some time in prison for misdemeanor assault and probation violation before trying to start his life again away from the public eye. He makes some appearances on behalf of his old team, the New York Jets, but he does not speak about his time in boxing.

George and Erin live in Bradenton, George with his partner, Holly, and Erin with her daughters, Kailey and Paige. They are no more than a five-minute drive from each other, and only an hour's trip from Hardee.

Erin's story in its way is more remarkable than Tim's, and she and her brother still have the thread that joins them. Tim's brothers Darrin and Tommy have families of their own too, and their visits to Hardee are great events for the Andersons.

Soon after Tim went to jail, his girlfriend Susan came to see him. For an hour they talked and held hands. Their goodbye was unspoken, but they both understood.

Jim Murphy lost his faith in the justice system and the media following the *60 Minutes* show and Tim's trial. He found a handbook containing lists of movie producers, and for a year he worked his way down it, telling them Tim Anderson's story. Several showed interest until they realised that there was no Hollywood ending. Jim split with his fiancée as the case took over his life. He only let it go when he realised that if he didn't it would cost him everything else. He finds it hard to talk about, even now.

Operation Dirty Gloves, the FBI's investigation into Rick Parker and fixed boxing matches, was dropped after Rick's death. Bill and Trish were denied access to most of the information it held when Tim came to trial four years later.

Doctor Donald Chumley, the ringside physician at Tim's

second fight with Mark, was one of the first medics on the scene when a bomb exploded at the Murrah Building, just around the corner from his office in Oklahoma City. Not long afterwards, he was piloting his plane, alone, back from a hunting trip when he lost control and crashed. His death got caught up in arguments made by Oklahoma Bomb conspiracy theorists, who believed that the FBI, and not Timothy McVeigh, caused the explosion.

Rob Russen decided to stay well away from boxing promotion. He found another job and enjoys his life in the Florida sun. In his spare time, he promotes fairs and shows with the old-time wrestling stars, where they sign autographs and meet their fans. He remains good friends with Derrick 'Starfire' Dukes, and he has just finished working on a website development project for his old foe, Don King.

Don Hazelton retired from the Florida State Athletic Commission after a decade as Executive Director, with the state acknowledged as one of the safest and best-regulated in America. He owns a restaurant in central Florida.

At one point in 2007, all of the major heavyweight belts were held by white men. It was the least lucrative time in the history of the division.

# Acknowledgments

I had never heard of Tim Anderson or Rick Parker until I read a wire report by Ken Rodriguez of the *Miami Herald* in a newspaper office in 1999. I first wrote to Tim in 2004 and we met in 2007. Throughout, I believe he has been truthful, honest and totally open, sometimes to his own detriment, and my first thanks go to him.

This book would not have been possible without Tim's friendship, or without the following people: George Anderson, Erin Anderson-O'Brock, Diane McVay, Jim Murphy, Rob Russen, Sharon Cobb, Bill McClellan, Patricia Cashman, Suzanne Migdall, Don Hazelton, Jack Solloway, Steve Canton, Randy Gerber, Ken Rodriguez and Bob Mladinich. All agreed to be interviewed at length, some of them several times, and also took follow-up phone calls, replied to emails, provided photographs and contact numbers and, in the case of Tim's family, opened up their houses and their lives, too. Rob Russen also made available the manuscript to his book *8 . . . 9 . . . 10 . . . You're Out*, which includes various faxes and communications relating to his time at Rick Parker

Presents . . . Sharon Cobb offered an invaluable journalist's insight, and Steve Canton gave the benefit of his years in boxing and all of his contacts. He and Randy Gerber provided fight footage, as did Vic Wysocki. The author and boxing writer Bob Mladinich made copies of the trial transcript and offered expert advice on boxing and the law. Trish Cashman and Bill McClellan spoke in great detail, explaining both points of law and their own feelings and emotions about Tim and his case, and made their papers available. Marty Sammon, Brian Garry, Kevin Finn, Derek Williams, Berry Tramel and Steve Thomasson also gave interviews, Jonathan Rendall offered memories of his investigations into Rick Parker, and Clint Calkins provided several useful contacts. Others spoke off the record, and thanks go to them, too.

A major contribution was made by Mary Lynn Canton, who worked for many weeks finding and reading documents, replying to emails, taking calls and clarifying many aspects of Tim's case, all unpaid. She and Steve Canton also travelled to Orlando to visit the offices of Trish Cashman and Bill McClellan to locate and copy papers relating to Tim's case. Thanks for everything, Mary Lynn.

I'd like to acknowledge the following newspapers, books, websites, publications and papers:

*Newspapers and news reports*
*Orlando Sentinel*, archives, 1986–99
*Miami Herald*, archives, 1986–99

*Major articles*
'The fix was in', William Nack and Sonja Steptoe, *Sports Illustrated*, 1993
'Hazelton fights boxing to clean up its corner', Brian Schmitz, *Orlando Sentinel*, 1993
'Boxing promoter faces his biggest fight out of the ring', Gerard Shields and Barry Cooper, *Orlando Sentinel*, 1994

'Rick "Elvis" Parker keeps his chin up', Barry Cooper, *Orlando Sentinel*, 1994

'A fighter in the corner: Don Hazelton is Florida boxing', Gerard Shields, *Orlando Sentinel*, 1995

'Ex-boxer faces biggest fight of his life', Gerard Shields, *Orlando Sentinel*, 1996

'Getting back on his feet, Barch won't take dive tonight', Ken Rodriguez, *Miami Herald*, 1997

'King's pawns', Howard Altman, *Philadelphia Citypaper*, 1997

'Fight fixer who lived the high life took the ultimate hit', Ken Rodriguez, *Miami Herald*, 1999

'Boxing tainted by the fix', Ken Rodriguez, *Miami Herald*, 1999

'Where the lions are afraid of the rats', Jack Newfield, *New York Sun*, 2004

'Clemency for Tim "Doc" Anderson', Robert Mladinich, *Sweet Science*, 2005

'Gastineau ready to put his (track) record behind him', Greg Garber, *ESPN*, 2005

*Books*
*Muhammad Ali: His Life and Times*, Thomas Hauser (Pan)
*The Life and Crimes of Don King*, Jack Newfield (Virgin)
*This Bloody Mary is the Last Thing I Own*, Jonathan Rendall (Faber)
*8 . . . 9 . . . 10 . . . You're Out*, Rob Russen (Rob Russen)

*Websites*
www.boxrec.com
www.thesweetscience.com

*Publications and papers*
State of Florida v Timothy Allen Anderson (transcript of trial, plus depositions, discoveries and various court papers,

and papers from the offices of Patricia Cashman and Bill McClellan, 1995–6)

Report of Autopsy on Richard Lynn Parker, Office of the Medical Examiner, District Nine, Orlando, Florida, 1995

The Boxer and the Death Penalty – The Media Factor in a Death Penalty Case, Margaret A. Mackenzie (Professional Profiles)

United States Court of Appeals for the Sixth Circuit, Randall Craig Cobb v Time Inc/*Sports Illustrated*, 2002

Cobb v *Sports Illustrated*: Actual Malice Requires More than Negligence, Allison Van Laningham (Smith Moore LLP)

Author's correspondence with Tim Anderson, 2004–2008

*Television*
'TKO', Steve Kroft, CBS *60 Minutes*, 1994

*Fight footage*
Tim Anderson v George Foreman (1987); v Pierre Coetzer (1988); v Larry Holmes (1991); v Mark Gastineau i and ii (both 1992)

Bert Cooper v Evander Holyfield (1991); v Michael Moorer (1992)

Tex Cobb v Sonny Barch (1992)

Mark Gastineau v Derrick Dukes (1991)

George Foreman v Tommy Morrison (1993); v Michael Moorer (1994)

Plus assorted newspaper and magazine reports 1986–94

Also:

Lucy Luck and Tristan Jones, who have taken a chance. Writing is a selfish occupation, and so all my love and thanks go to Ruby Hotten, Lily Hotten, George Hotten, Maureen Hotten, Julie Simpson, Caroline Cope and my friends Mick Wall, Paul Elliott, Richard Bath and Iain Fletcher, and everyone else who had to hear about it.

Finally, to Yasmin Hounsell, who has been more than my girlfriend and best friend; she was there all the way through Florida, chasing the trails of men she had never met right up to room 250 of the Embassy Suites, where half of this story ended and the other half began.

Tim Anderson would like to acknowledge the following people:

My love and appreciation to my wonderful family for the support I've received my entire life. To my late mother, Jacqueline Mundo Anderson, whom I adored. To my late grandparents Alice and George Anderson and Barbara, and Alex Mundo, my rock and still going strong at ninety-six. To my awesome dad George Anderson and Holly Chaney, my sister Erin and Adam O'Brock and their lovely young ladies Kailey and Paige. My brother Tom and Pam Anderson and sons Brad and Bryant, my brother Darrin and Kristi Anderson, Tyler, Emily and Lizzie.

The other people who made an impact on my life: my best friends James 'Jimbo' Murphy, Diane McVay and Clint Calkins.

To all of my friends and supporters in boxing, my opponents in my career and my trainers and training partners, Alan and Suzanne Migdall, Kevin Finn, Billy Cotter, Jackie Kallan, Vinnie Paz, Susan Scully, Chaplain McGahey, Marcia Silvers and crew, Diane Berry, Diane and Jamin Morse, Marty Sammon, Bruce 'The Mouse' Strauss, Janell and the Missouri girls, Jerry 'Fists of Fury' Sitzes, D-Nice, Josh, Billy, Dion and Bill, Cuz and Jimbo, Lou Gerber, Joe Derrick, Marty Sammon and Steve Canton. May you rest in peace, Rick Parker.

A very special thanks to my angel, Mary Lynn McDavid, and to the janitor who saved my life on 4 December 1992 in Oklahoma.

This book is a work of non-fiction, based on the interviews and research alluded to here. All of those interviewees have their version of the story; this one is mine alone. Where recollections of undocumented events have differed, I have tried to follow their most obvious course. Unrecorded dialogue has been modelled as closely as possible on the memories of those involved. Rick Parker's interior monologues are based on the views, feelings and emotions he made known, and, of course, on his character and subsequent actions.